History of Modern Furniture

Karl Mang

History of Modern Furniture

Translated by John William Gabriel

Harry N. Abrams, Inc., Publishers, New York

Editor: Bitite Vinklers

Library of Congress Cataloging in Publication Data
Mang, Karl, 1922-
    History of modern furniture.
    Translation of Geschichte des modernen Möbels.
    Includes bibliographical references and
index.
    1. Furniture—History—19th century.
2. Furniture—History—20th century.
I. Title.
NK2385.M3613   749.2′04   79-11551
ISBN 0-8109-1066-7

Library of Congress Catalog Card Number: 79-11551

© 1978 Verlag Gerd Hatje, Stuttgart

Printed and bound in Japan

Contents

For Eva, Bauxi, Carolina, and Hannerl

List of Illustrations

Furniture As an Expression of Its Age

Anonymous Furniture in the Nineteenth Century—
Harbingers of the Machine Aesthetic

43. French garden chair

44. Luigi Elli. Theater seats

45. Catalogue page of the Société Anonyme des Hauts-Fourneaux & Fonderies du Val d'Osne

46. Cowley & James, Walsall. Brass bed

47. Chair and stool of cast iron

48. Garden bench of cast iron, with fern motif on backrest

49. English rocking chair of cast iron, with velvet upholstery

50. Wheelchair

51. Dining table and chairs, after a United States patent of 1889

52. G. Wilson. Drawing of folding chair of iron, after a United States patent of 1871

53. G. Wilson. Folding chair of iron, after a United States patent of 1871

54. Dentist chair, after a United States patent of 1879

55. Chair, after a United States patent of 1853

56. Armchair, after a United States patent of 1874

57. George M. Pullman. Dining car, after a United States patent of 1869

58. J.S. van den Abeele. *Salon of Villa Paolina with Zenaide Bonaparte and Her Children*

59. Emanuele Rambaldi. Chair

60. Giovanni Battista Ravenna. Chair

61. Lathe-turned chair from Chiavari

62. Gio Ponti. Chair

63. Toilet scene on a Roman sepulcher, found in Neumagen an der Mosel

64. Exhibition opening, Weimar, 1904

65. Wicker chair

66. Nanna Ditzel. Chair and stool of Spanish cane

67. Egon Eiermann. Basket chair of Spanish cane

68. Living room with wicker furniture in an American home

69. Michael Thonet. Armchair

70. Bending wood in a Thonet factory

71. Page from the Thonet Brothers' catalogue

72. Michael Thonet. Three upholstered chairs in bentwood technique and parquet floors for Palais Liechtenstein, Vienna

73. Carl Leistler. Upholstered chair

74. Michael Thonet. Chair, armchair, bench, and table of rosewood; and table with brass inlays. For the Great Exhibition in London, 1851

75. Thonet Chair No. 1 (early version)

76. Thonet Chair No. 4 (early version)

77. Thonet Chair No. 4 (version with leg ring and reinforcement of the back legs)

78. Thonet Chair No. 6

79. Thonet Chair No. 13

80. Thonet Chair No. 16

81. Thonet Chair No. 18

82. Thonet Chair No. 56

83. Thonet Chair No. 221

84. Chair, "woven" of three lengths of wood

85. Thonet chair, made of one continuous piece of molded wood

86. Thonet Chair No. 14

87, 88. Tools for bending backrests and seat frames

89. Ferdinand Fellner, Jr. The Thonet House on Stephansplatz, Vienna

90. Office furniture, Thonet catalogue of 1911 and 1915 supplement

91. Child's cradle, Thonet catalogue

92. Desk Chair No. 6009 (later Thonet-Mundus B 9)

93. Thonet Wardrobe No. 10.907a (known as a wall clothes rack)

The Theories of William Morris and the Challenge of Industry

141. Victor Horta. Stairwell, Hôtel Tassel, Brussels

142. Workshop of the Société van de Velde in Ixelles

143. Henri van de Velde. Dining room in the house of Harry Graf Kessler, Weimar

144. Henri van de Velde. Sewing table and armchair

145. Henri van de Velde. Dining-room chair with wicker seat in Haus Bloemenwerf, Uccle, Brussels

146. Henri van de Velde. Desk

147. Henri van de Velde. Gentleman's study, Haus Hohenhof, Hagen, Westphalia

148. Henri van de Velde. Lady's sitting room, Haus Hohenhof, Hagen, Westphalia

149. Hector Guimard. Bedroom

150. Hector Guimard. Desk, designed for his own house

151. Eugène Gaillard. Cabinet

152. Émile Gallé. Bedroom

153. Émile Gallé. Lady's writing desk

154. Eugène Vallin. Dining room

155. Louis Majorelle. Small table

156. Charles Rennie Mackintosh. Dining room in the house of an artlover

157. Charles Rennie Mackintosh. Reception room and music room in the house of an artlover

158. Charles Rennie Mackintosh. Reading room in the library of the Glasgow School of Art, as originally furnished with Mackintosh's version of the Windsor chair

159. Charles Rennie Mackintosh. Chair, probably from the Cranston Tearoom

160. Charles Rennie Mackintosh. Entry hall of Hill House, Helensburgh

161. Joseph Maria Olbrich. Music room in Das Neue Palais, Darmstadt

162. Joseph Maria Olbrich. Children's furniture from the princess's house at Schloss Wolfsgarten near Darmstadt

163. Josef Hoffmann. Corner of a living room, from *Ver Sacrum 1898–1903*

164. Josef Hoffmann. Bedroom in a converted farmhouse, Bergerhöhe bei Hohenberg, Lower Austria

165. Bernhard Pankok. Music salon, created for the World Exhibition, Saint Louis, 1904

166. August Endell. Bookcase

167. Bernhard Pankok. Sketch

168. Bruno Paul. Dining room, exhibited in Dresden, 1906

169. Richard Riemerschmid. Armchair, painted red

170. Hermann Obrist. Chairs and serving table, from a dining-room set

171. Antoni Gaudí. Chair from Casa Calvet

172. Antoni Gaudí. Bench from the private apartment of the owner of Casa Battló, Barcelona

173. Antoni Gaudí. Dining room in Casa Battló, Barcelona

174. Antoni Gaudí. Casa Milá, Barcelona, floor plan

175. Antoni Gaudí. Chaise longue, Palacio Güell, Barcelona

176. Frank Lloyd Wright. Armchair

177. Frank Lloyd Wright. Living room of the Avery Coonley House, Riverside, Illinois

178. Frank Lloyd Wright. Preliminary drawing for the Avery Coonley House, Riverside, Illinois

179. Otto Wagner. The Green Room (Vice-Governor's Office), Post Office Savings Bank, Vienna

180. Otto Wagner. Conference room, Post Office Savings Bank, Vienna

181. Adolf Loos. Dining nook in the large living room, Haus Steiner, Vienna

182. Adolf Loos. Extendable table and matching chair

183. Adolf Loos. "My wife's bedroom," Loos apartment, Vienna

184. Adolf Loos. Die Kärntner Bar (American Bar), Vienna

185. Josef Hoffmann. Small desk

186. Koloman Moser. Dining-room furnishings

187. Josef Hoffmann. Dining room, Palais Stoclet, Brussels

188. Josef Hoffmann. Nook with fountain in the hall of Palais Stoclet, Brussels

From De Stijl to International Style

232. Walter Gropius. Lounge with coffee shop in the German Pavilion, International Exhibition, Paris, 1930

233. Marcel Breuer. Chair without back legs

234. Mart Stam. Chair without back legs, Model "S 34"

235. Ludwig Mies van der Rohe. Chair without back legs, Model "MR"

236. Marcel Breuer with Alfred and Emil Roth. Small apartment houses at Doldertal, Zurich

237. Marcel Breuer. Dining room, Piscator House, Berlin

238. Ludwig Mies van der Rohe. Design for the Gericke House, Berlin

239. Hans Scharoun. Schminke House, Löbau, Silesia

240. Ludwig Mies van der Rohe. German Pavilion, International Exhibition, Barcelona, 1929

241. Ludwig Mies van der Rohe. Chair of the "MR" type. "Brno" chair. "Barcelona" chair

242. Ludwig Mies van der Rohe. Living room, Tugendhat House, Brno

243. Ludwig Mies van der Rohe. Chair without back legs

244. Le Corbusier and Pierre Jeanneret. Hall of the Pavillon de l'Esprit Nouveau, Exposition Internationale des Arts Décoratifs, Paris, 1925

245. Le Corbusier and Pierre Jeanneret. Exterior of Villa Savoye, Poissy

246. Le Corbusier and Pierre Jeanneret. Living room on the first floor with roof terrace, Villa Savoye, Poissy

247. Le Corbusier. A house in Carthage

248. Le Corbusier. Library in the Church House, Ville d'Avray

249. Le Corbusier, Pierre Jeanneret, Charlotte Perriand. Table

250. Le Corbusier, Pierre Jeanneret, Charlotte Perriand. Fully adjustable chaise longue

251. Le Corbusier, Pierre Jeanneret, Charlotte Perriand. Armchair with pivoting backrest

252. Le Corbusier, Pierre Jeanneret, Charlotte Perriand. "Fauteuil grand confort"

253. Ernst May and E. Kaufmann. Living room in the Praunheim Project, Frankfurt am Main

254. Exhibition by the Württemberg Committee in the Municipal Housing Project at Stuttgart-Wangen

255. Ferdinand Kramer. Desk with two drawers; stool with canework seat

256. Ferdinand Kramer. Occasional tables which may be folded or extended

257. Ferdinand Kramer. Sideboard

258. Ferdinand Kramer. Dining room of suburban house by J.J.P. Oud

259. Franz Schuster. Living room in a project house, Frankfurt am Main

260. Franz Schuster. Corner in a living room of a project house, Frankfurt am Main

261. Grete Schütte-Lihotzky. "Frankfurt Kitchen"

262. Grete Schütte-Lihotzky. One-room apartment of a working woman, Frankfurt am Main

Scandinavian Furniture—from Anonymity to World Renown

263. Carl Malmsten. Cabinet

264. Josef Frank. Desk

265. Drawing from the *Möbelråd* handbook published by Svenska Slöjdföreningen, 1961

266. Erik Gunnar Asplund. Werkbund Exhibition, Stockholm, 1930

267. Bruno Mathsson. Own summer house in Frösakull, Holland

268. Bruno Mathsson. Design for club chair with webbing seat and back

269. Bruno Mathsson. The three basic forms of the Mathsson chair

270. Bruno Mathsson. Armchair for a hospital

271. Bruno Mathsson. Chair with armrests

272. Bruno Mathsson. Study chair with high back

273. Knud Friis and Elmar Moltke Nielsen. Living room in a Danish one-family house

274. Kaare Klint. Sideboard

275. Dining room, with furniture by Kaare Klint

Furniture Design After World War II

326. Eero Saarinen. Easy chair and stool

327, 328. Eero Saarinen. Chairs and table

329. Florence Knoll Bassett. Furnishings for the reception room, office of the Connecticut General Life Insurance Company, Bloomfield, Connecticut

330. Dining room, with "Brno" chairs by Mies van der Rohe and a table by Eero Saarinen

331. Robert Haussmann. Chair

332. Tobia Scarpa: "Bastiano" sofa. Vico Magistretti: "Caori" table

333. Arne Jacobsen. Office of the City Engineer in Glostrup City Hall

334. Arne Jacobsen and Niels Jørgen Haugesen. "Djob" office-furniture program

335. Poul Kjaerholm. Sofa

336. Poul Kjaerholm. Chair

337. Hans Gugelot. "M 125" modular group

338. Jørn Utzon. Portable furniture system

339. Jørn Utzon. Chair and footstool

340. Franco Albini. Rocking chair

341. Agnoldomenico Pica. Chair

342. Giuseppe Terragni. Chair

343. Franco Albini. Radio mounted between two pieces of plate glass

344. Luigi Figini and Gino Pollini. Design for a combination radio and record player

345. Giovanni Pintori. Poster for Olivetti typewriter

346. Luisa Castiglioni and Margherita Mori. Living room with bookcase, work table, and chaise longue

347. Angelo Mangiarotti. Bookcase, fitted together of separate wooden elements

348. Franco Albini, Luigi Colombini, and Enzio Sgrelli. Armchair

349. Angelo Mangiarotti. Wardrobe, built up of various-sized elements

350. Franco Albini and Franca Helg. Armchair

351. Osvaldo Borsani. Armchair

352. Marco Zanuso and Richard Sapper. Armchair

353. Marco Zanuso and Richard Sapper. Children's chair

354. Vico Magistretti. "Selene" stacking chair

355. Joe C. Colombo. Stacking chair

356. Carlo Viganò. Modular cabinet series

357. Anna Castelli Ferrieri. Round plastic containers

358, 359. Pierluigi Molinari. "Box System"

360. Mies van der Rohe. Design of a seat shell to be made of plastic

361. Vico Magistretti. Table, with detachable legs; chairs

362. Corrado Cocconi and Fabio Lenci. Shelf system with Plexiglas cubes

363. Jürgen Lange: "behr 1600" wall unit. Mario Bellini: "Amanta" stacking table. Verner Panton: stacking chair

364. A living room

365. Jürgen Lange. "behr 1600 paneel" program

366. A spacious living room in a private American home

367. Living room with freely grouped seating elements

368–370. Joe C. Colombo. "Additional System" seating program

371. Joe C. Colombo. Kitchen box block

372. Joe C. Colombo. Central living block for "Wohnmodell 1969"

373. Olivier Mourgue. "Wohnmodell 1972"

374, 375. Alberto Rosselli with Abe Kozo. "Pack 1" portable folding chair

376, 377. Günter Sulz. "Canvas" seating combination

378, 379. Maurizio Dallasta and Davide Mercatali. "Nomade" chair

380. Piero Gatti, Cesare Paolini, Franco Teodoro. Seat bag

381. Rolf Heide. "Roll cabinets"

382. Jonathan De Pas, Donato D'Urbino, Paolo Lomazzi. "Dado & Vite" furniture system

383. Günter Renkel. "Robinson" program

Foreword

This book is not an impartial, disinterested view of the history of modern furniture. I have not hesitated to choose, from the abundant production of the past 150 years, only those tendencies that have proved to be more than short-lived fashions.

The connection between the Industrial Revolution and social change, between the emergence of a new social stratum and the search for a style suited to its needs, between the development of industrial mass production and the social forces it has released—these questions stand at the beginning of the book, which emphasizes the positive aspects of the past century and a half in furniture design and attempts to present them for modern eyes.

This period saw many and diverse aesthetic and social theories, and many attempts on the part of architects and designers to create furniture and housing for the needs of a rapidly industrialized world. The abundance of new ideas has indeed been so great that there is every reason to believe that today we should be living in an era of a perfectly designed human environment. This, as we all know, is not the case. Most people still have no real feeling for good furniture or good design in their personal surroundings and live in a world of *kitsch* produced by lack of interest, lack of understanding, perhaps lack of knowledge—and certainly the desire to maximize profits.

This book has a position to defend. It was written as a challenge to all those who prefer the mediocrity of imitation to the great achievements of creative design, who would rather juggle with slick forms than engage in demanding research.

It could not have been written without the investigations of the many art historians and theoreticians of modern architecture who have contributed to our understanding of the subject, particularly as it relates to the nineteenth century. The bibliography at the end, though it makes no pretense to exhaustiveness, will perhaps point the way to all those—be they architects, designers, or laymen—who wish to pursue the subject of furniture design beyond these pages.

Gerd Hatje deserves much of the praise if this book helps to turn people's interest away from the nostalgia of Historicism to a courageous reappraisal of what our own epoch has to offer. My special thanks go to my wife, without whose help in our architecture office I would not have found the time to complete this project. To the publisher and to Frau Dr. Charlotte Blauensteiner of the Österreichisches Institut für Formgebung I would like to express my gratitude for their valuable suggestions in reading the manuscript.

Karl Mang

Furniture As an Expression of Its Age

The development of modern furniture parallels that of modern architecture and modern technology. The American Declaration of Independence of 1776 and the Bill of Rights, the first spinning machine driven by water power (installed in 1775 by Sir Richard Arkwright in the first "modern" factory at Nottingham), and the storming of the Bastille in 1789 mark the beginning of a fundamental change in our world that is still going on today. In the twentieth century this process of change has taken the form of a conflict between capitalism and communism, but also that of a quest for social justice within each of these systems. The social transformations we have witnessed, which have been further complicated by the political coming-of-age of the Third World, are the framework within which all of man's activities take place, within which we build and live.

Like architecture, furniture and home furnishings may symbolize the rise to power of a class, a social stratum, or a nation. Indeed, they are very precise barometers, for they react rapidly and sensitively to social changes otherwise almost imperceptible. Furniture and the rooms it is used in are so much a part of their owners that they indicate their social position and relation to others in a very direct way. Furniture is a key to both public and private personalities—the cabinet by André Charles Boulle (Plate 1), with its stark shapes and magnificent intarsia work, stands just as clearly for the absolute power of Louis XIV as a modest bentwood chair by Thonet does for the anonymous consumer of the new age (Plate 2).

As the nineteenth century was getting under way, the styles of Classicism and Empire threw a last backward glance at the glory of the *ancien régime*. The flowing robes in the paintings by Jacques Louis David (Plate 3) and the Greek and Roman motifs on the furniture of the time (Plate 4) speak the same message of imperial power and a desire to regain the lost serenity of a classical age. The impression is heightened by the glossy surfaces of the dark mahogany veneer and the imposing volume of these pieces—though their technical perfection is the result of the first factory-based production methods.

With the furniture and interiors of the Biedermeier period we see a first, halting step toward modern design (Plate 5). Born of a reduction of Classical and Empire ornament and the need to adapt furniture to the more modest dimensions of the bourgeois parlor, this style soon proved to have a life and power very much its own. The organic shapes of Biedermeier chairs and sofas herald a functionalism that became possible when people began to turn their backs on finery and show. Modest, light, and friendly rooms with unprepossessing furniture exuded peace and order and seemed to lend this style, which was mainly Central European, something lasting and final. The peace was deceptive, however; beneath the surface of Metternich's political order deep social and economic unrest was brewing. Middle-class society had been terribly frightened by the events of the French Revolution and felt safe under the wing of its monarchs. People's homes were their fortresses, where their wives, children, and friends waited to comfort and enfold them in that atmosphere which has entered the German language with the adjective *biedermeierlich*.

In the country of earliest industrialization, England, people held tenaciously to the

1. André Charles Boulle. Cabinet. c. 1700. The Louvre, Paris.
Boulle, *ébéniste du Roy,* designed and made furniture whose simple, basic forms were often decorated with inlay work in tortoise shell and brass or pewter (Boulle technique).

2

3

4

3. Jacques Louis David. *Madame Réca-mier*. 1800. The Louvre, Paris.
Classic Roman motifs abound in the style known as Empire, which came in about 1795 under the *Directoire* and reached its peak with the rule of Napoleon.

4. Music room at Malmaison Castle near Paris. c. 1800. Decor by Charles Percier and Pierre F.L. Fontaine; furniture by Jacob Frères.
Every detail of rooms such as this one is infused with the spirit of ancient Rome—which is probably what gives Empire such great unity as a style.

◁ 2. Michael Thonet. Chair No. 14.
This model went into production in 1859; by 1930 almost fifty million had been made.

5

5. Leopold Kupelwieser. *Tableau Performed by the Schubert Circle at Atzenbrugg (Expulsion from Paradise)*. 1821. Watercolor. Historisches Museum der Stadt Wien. Smooth surfaces and lack of decoration are characteristic of the Biedermeier style. Its comfortable furniture and light-filled rooms were the height of bourgeois living during the nineteenth century.

styles of furnishing created by the three great English craftsmen of the eighteenth century: Thomas Chippendale, Thomas Sheraton, and George Hepplewhite (Plate 7). For the rest the motto was Back to Nature—a desire that found its expression all over Europe in the idyllic landscapes of Romantic painting. The bourgeoisie spent their hours in country houses dotted over the broad, green counties. In the Midlands, meanwhile, narrow, dirty industrial towns had begun to spring up; the smokestacks of the first factories to spout smoke; and the fleet, sailing under the ensign of laissez faire, had begun to take advantage of a new freedom of the seas to bring back raw materials to feed the machines (Plate 6). As the feudal order declined and workingmen were released from the land to stream into the centers of new industry, the ruling classes continued to live in consciously historical surroundings. Neo-Gothic was a reminder of the English nobility's glorious past that not even the new factory owners could resist (Plates 8, 9).

While Early Victorian England was enjoying its country idyll, in Munich in 1816 Leo von Klenze began to build a row of Neoclassic houses along Ludwigstrasse, reaching right out from the petty-bourgeois quarters into the green suburbs. And not far from Vienna, about an hour by horse-drawn carriage, a town of villas and spas arose in a cross between Biedermeier and Neoclassic styles—the town of Baden,

6

6. Karl Friedrich Schinkel. Sketch of Manchester. 1826.
Huge factories and warehouses, usually built of red brick, dominated the English industrial towns of the nineteenth century.

7. English rolltop desk with bookcase. c. 1790. Victoria and Albert Museum, London.
The furniture of this period is characterized by extremely practical design and reserved decor.

8. Richard Norman Shaw. Neo-Gothic bureau with bookcase. c. 1860. Victoria and Albert Museum, London.
A combination of quality craftsmanship and medieval form was considered by many to be an antidote to the shoddiness of early industrial products.

7　　　　　　　　　　　　8

9. William and Separ Owen. Houses for Port Sunlight. c. 1890.
Historical borrowings are still evident in this first attempt to build housing for working-men and their families in the vicinity of the factory.

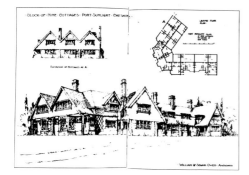

which had been destroyed by fire, was given a new face by the architect Josef Kornhäusel.

The fact that most of the European political leaders of the time were economically progressive despite their basic conservatism probably was due to the insight that economic prosperity had a stabilizing effect; perhaps this explains why Chancellor Metternich brought a man like Michael Thonet to Vienna. Thonet's first bentwood chairs were built for the palaces of his noble patrons, only much later becoming furniture for the masses. The official state arts of painting and architecture, embedded in Historicism, made no attempt to reflect the new era in creative terms. And the laboring class was too deeply involved in a battle for sheer survival to be concerned with aesthetic matters.

Rapid technical progress, the invention of new manufacturing methods, and the introduction of new materials could not long be ignored by traditional craftsmen. Even André Charles Boulle, the great *ébéniste* of Louis XIV France, had heard of division of labor, and even the most illustrious of the French cabinetmaking firms and David Roentgen's enterprise in the Rhineland were already organized according to this new principle. It was here, if very gradually, that the transition from artisanry to industry was made.

As these small firms began to grow, their owners began to organize sales and distribution along modern lines, too. In Vienna the Dannhauser furniture factory already employed 130 workers by 1808, and a short time later they had begun to offer their furniture and housewares for sale at the premises and in nearby salesrooms. As traditional cabinetmakers, however, they continued to see their task as filling the Historicist rooms of historically inspired buildings with furniture of every imaginable style (Plate 10). And since their work was exquisitely crafted, despite its debt to past styles, it found favor with the theoreticians and the newly established museums—the Victoria and Albert Museum in London and the Museum für Kunst und Industrie in Vienna.

In this world of rapid social change and aesthetic nostalgia, two achievements

10

stand out—aside from experiments with the new material, iron—as prefiguring the industrialized future. These were the furniture of the American Shakers (Plate 11) and the bentwood chairs of Michael Thonet (Plate 12). The Shakers, in the late eighteenth century, over a hundred years before Adolf Loos, rejected all decoration in architecture, household goods, and furniture for moral and religious reasons; bentwood chairs, because they were technically innovative and cheap to produce, became the model of furniture for a mass society and an ideal for furniture designers up to the present day.

Technical improvements left their strongest mark on American design. Despite the fact that American industrialization lagged behind the English (the first American cotton-spinning mill was built in Pawtucket in 1793), more highly developed capitalist production methods soon made up for lost time. By the latter half of the nineteenth century most manual labor in factories had been replaced by machine work. Simple furniture that hitherto had been made entirely by hand was now produced, piece by piece, with the aid of machines.

Experiments with new materials and approaches led to a spate of patents (Plate 13)—for example, for mechanized office furniture that anticipated much that was to come. Strangely enough, these technical innovations had almost no influence on furniture style in general. Not even the eminently practical and variable mechanical

11. Shaker furniture. ▷
The Shakers took over their furniture forms and production methods from New England Colonial, and they remained true to them from the late-eighteenth to the mid-nineteenth century. In the Shakers we see the Puritan ethic at its clearest.

12. Michael Thonet. Bentwood chairs. ▷
The development of bentwood furniture from the mid-nineteenth century is a good example of the way a new manufacturing method can lead to a new formal language. The forms were reduced to their simplest terms (Chair No. 14, Plate 2) only when mass production got under way.

◁10. Study in the Grützner Villa, Munich.
1884.
The overloaded grandeur and stylistic confusion of this interior is a good example of how most people wanted to live at the close of the nineteenth century.

contrivances that made railroad travel across the vast American continent more comfortable than ever before, with the famous Pullman cars, had the power to change the average American's idea of home furnishings. Perhaps there is a parallel here with the tall office buildings of Chicago (Plate 14), which also represent a very early attempt to create something truly new in architecture, and which were also virtually neglected for decades; only very recently have these pioneering achievements begun to affect architectural thinking with their open plans, large areas of glass, elevators, and central heating.

To most citizens of the young American nation the freedom of the pioneer soon came to mean the freedom to make money, which is probably why America developed so differently in social terms than Europe. The implications of buildings

11

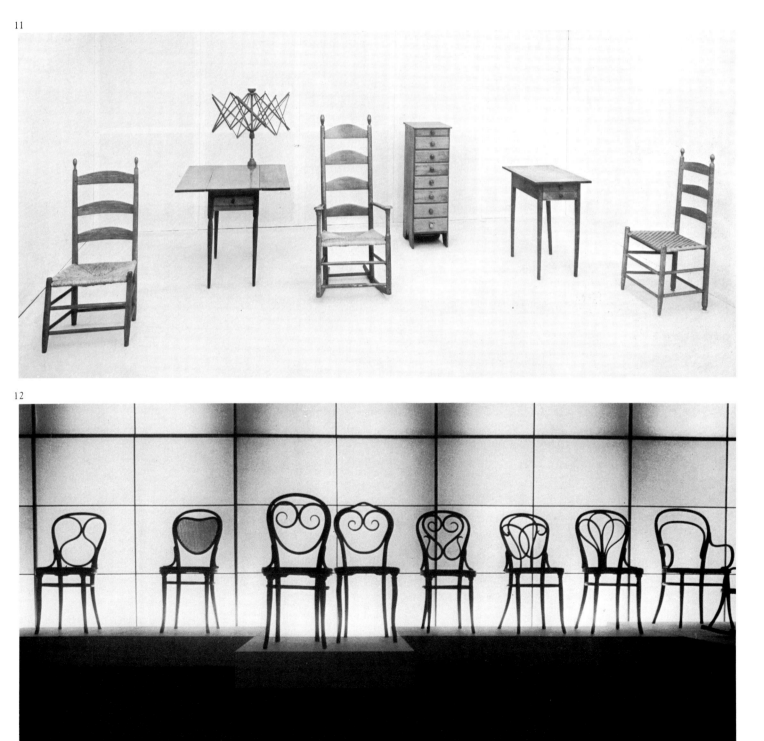

12

like those of Louis Sullivan (Plate 14) or the houses and furniture of Frank Lloyd Wright (Plate 16) have never been adequately appreciated in the United States. For the self-made man, prosperous businessman, and self-confident technocrat, culture was something that had to be imported from Europe. With historical furniture came old paintings and ancient relics, all of which are still on view today in places like the Morgan Library or the Frick Collection in New York—an unchanging testimony to the taste of America's high society at the close of the century.

If things took a different turn in Europe, it was largely due to men like John Ruskin and William Morris. Morris, who extolled the virtues of medieval craftsmanship and hated the evils of industrialization, laid the groundwork for a new renaissance in design. Central to his thinking was the belief in quality work, which he felt could be achieved only through the cooperation of artist and craftsman; he was also a convinced socialist. If he opposed technical development it was for moral reasons: to him art for all was just as important as freedom for all. Both his writings and his works were key factors in the search that began in the late nineteenth century for new methods and forms commensurate with the new age (Plate 15). His ideal of a community of artists and craftsmen became a reality with such groups as the Werkstätten founded about the turn of the century in Vienna and Munich, and his social and ethical concerns carried over, half a century later, to the Bauhaus School in Weimar.

In looking at the developments in nineteenth-century design and attempting to reduce them to a few important terms, we can discern two parallel paths. On the one hand we have technical progress with its acceptance of new materials and continual improvement of production methods, of which an example would be Thonet's bentwood chairs; on the other, the movement for artistic quality and social equality called into being by William Morris. These two lines of development had to go through many detours before they converged in the early twentieth century in groups such as the German Werkbund, many of whose ideas the Bauhaus was later to spread worldwide.

In this search for a new world of form, one of the stepping-stones was Art Nouveau, a style that helped overcome the impasse of Historicism (Plate 17). Though for a while many people mistook this stepping-stone for a wide thoroughfare, Art Nouveau was not really much of an advance on Morris's ideas in theory and made use of outmoded manufacturing methods in practice. For instance, Henri van de Velde's beautiful chairs, hand-carved of solid wood (Plate 18), though one might consider them the final flowering of an art, were certainly not good prototypes for mass production—they were simply too expensive for that. Between their ideal of social justice and the reality of furnishing the well-to-do homes, which these men were dependent on for their livelihood, yawned an unbridgeable gulf.

The world exhibitions held between 1851 and 1900 had a profound influence on interior design. Joseph Paxton's Crystal Palace at the Great Exhibition of 1851 in London was a revelation, in the way it destroyed the traditional boundary between exterior and interior space; subsequent exhibitions presented new mechanical inventions of all kinds to a wide public for the first time. Catalogues and newspaper articles helped spread the word, as did the numerous magazines on home furnishings that began to appear at about this time.

Our century brought with it a triumph of tradition. Despite experiments with new forms in furniture, time-tested middle-class taste remained basically unchallenged, whether in apartment buildings in town or in private houses in the suburbs. It would take a world war and the Russian Revolution to bring about the beginnings of a true re-evaluation, though the first signs had come earlier, in the shape of the German Werkbund, founded in 1907, with its attempts to integrate craftsmanship and indus-

13. Revolving chair in a saloon car, the Chicago–Kansas City Line. 1888.
The great distances to be covered on the American continent (and certainly competition among the railroads) made comfortable and versatile furnishings in trains a necessity.

14. Louis Sullivan. Carson, Pirie & Scott Store, Chicago. 1899 (expanded 1903–4).
In this building the relation between the facade and interior space is made visible: "Form follows function."

15. Morris & Co. The Green Dining Room. 1867. Stained-glass windows by Edward Burne-Jones. Victoria and Albert Museum, London.

The furnishings of this room represent the cooperation of architect, artist, and craftsman that was William Morris's goal. The Puritan faith of the Shakers has made way here for the utopia of early socialism.

16. Frank Lloyd Wright. Cheney House, Oak Park, Illinois. 1893.

"Organic architecture." Like Sullivan's buildings, Wright's houses developed from the inside out. He attempted to recreate a unity of architecture and furnishings that had not existed since the days of Biedermeier.

17. Victor Horta. Dining hall, Hôtel Solvay, Brussels. 1895–1900.
The proportions and decor of this room, with its tall windows, still owe much to the *palais* of the eighteenth century. And the chairs are much more decorative than those designed by Henri van de Velde at about the same time (Plate 18).

try, and with the work of Peter Behrens, who was responsible for architecture and design at the large German industrial firm AEG (Plates 19, 20).

The First World War changed everything. Particularly in the countries that were hardest hit by war and economic depression—Germany, Austria, and, of course, Russia—people began to question the value of traditional norms. Is it any wonder that they embraced utopian ideas, in the face of a reality that seemed almost impossible to master? Postwar German Expressionism, a movement that started in Berlin, attempted to put the dreams of a tormented age into concrete form in its designs for buildings and furnishings (Plates 21, 22). Though they spoke eloquently of their creators' hopes for society, the Expressionists' conceptions were technically impractical and thus had little power to change it.

A more rational approach was taken by the Bauhaus, located first in Weimar (from 1919 to 1925) and then in Dessau (1925 to 1932). Influenced as much by the Dutch De Stijl movement as by Russian Constructivism, the Bauhaus took decisive steps toward the integration of all the visual arts into society, particularly architecture. It worked out a new conception of interior space, with furnishings (Plate 24) that, similar to the Japanese tradition, made man the center of things again. Designers such as Marcel Breuer (Plate 25), Mies van der Rohe, and Mart Stam took advantage of new technology to create the chairs made of steel tubing that were to become a hallmark of the twenties. If later, particularly under the architect Hannes Meyer, the

18. Henri van de Velde. Dining room, Herbert Esche House, Karl-Marx-Stadt. 1897–98.

Historicism as a state of mind was not fully overcome until designers began to create interiors according to an overall conception that included even the most seemingly insignificant detail–down to lighting fixtures and doorknobs.

Bauhaus began to give precedence to social over aesthetic ideas, it was little more than a logical result of the privation that Germany had had to struggle with throughout that black decade.

Inexpensive furniture and functional housing for broad sectors of the population became the central task of the postwar period. In Vienna, under Social Democratic Mayors Jakob Reumann and Karl Seitz and their Treasurer Hugo Breitner, great numbers of low-cost apartments were built in answer to the speculative schemes of the prewar years (a program, by the way, that has not been studied nearly as carefully as it deserves). Franz Schuster was able to try out his ideas for prefabricated furniture for the first time here (Plate 23), and Grete Schütte-Lihotzky her kitchen designs. Both came to maturity in the Frankfurt settlements built under the direction of Ernst May.

In formal terms this epoch was one of Neue Sachlichkeit, and nowhere was the spirit of functionalism better represented than at the Werkbund exhibition of 1927 at Weissenhof in Stuttgart (Plate 26). The most important architects and designers of the age—men like Mies van der Rohe, Walter Gropius, J.J.P. Oud, Le Corbusier, and Hugo Häring—contributed exemplary housing schemes to it. This exhibition was perhaps the purest manifestation of the International Style in architecture ever—the buildings clean of line, the interiors simple, the furnishings frugal. Mies van der Rohe, whose conception of open interior space was to point the way for an entire generation of architects (Plate 30), was responsible for the exhibition. Since he more than anyone was the aesthete of the movement, the social component plays a secondary role in his work, though this cannot be said of the use to which his ideas have been put by his many students and followers. Le Corbusier designed two buildings for Weissenhof, which contained the seeds of ideas he was able to realize in full only later, after World War Two, in structures like his Unité d'Habitation in Marseilles.

By 1930 it seemed that modern architecture had carried the day all over Europe. But conservative forces were regrouping, and just a few years after the Weissenhof exhibition an "anti-settlement" was erected in the same city, Stuttgart (Plate 27), which was as technically conservative as its predecessor had been progressive, recommending the traditional German-style bungalow as the dwelling of the future.

In Russia, after a few early successes, the Constructivists were relegated to the architectural shadows. The pseudo-bourgeois period of Stalinist architecture had begun. It was a highly eclectic style, and its furnishings betrayed absolutely no traces of the revolutionary social change that had gone before. In Germany Hitler's *Blut und Boden* housing thrived, and the great names in architecture and painting were forced into exile. The brutal Neoclassicism of Albert Speer was well served by its monumental, pseudo-Renaissance furnishings (Plates 28, 29). Only in Italy did political reaction, allied with a young and developing industry, accept or at least tolerate modern design.

What was astonishing was that in all this America stood aside. Skyscrapers continued to go up with Gothic or Renaissance trimmings (Plate 32), and most furniture to be made in eclectic styles, or, for those who could afford it, the real thing was imported directly from the crumbling European market.

Thus by the outbreak of World War Two there had been a general retreat of modern architecture and furniture design. Neither Hitler's housing settlements nor Stalin's building activities contributed anything of note to contemporary living. In Central Europe the war interrupted developments for years—people living among

19

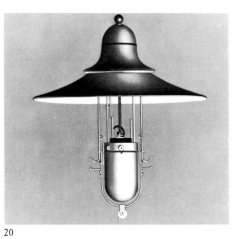

20

19. Peter Behrens. AEG turbine factory, Berlin. 1909.
This assembly building, with its huge expanses of glass, is at one and the same time eminently functional and an imposing symbol of a powerful corporation.

20. Peter Behrens. AEG arc lamp for indirect lighting. 1907.

21

22

23. Franz Schuster. *Aufbaumöbel* (unit furniture). Drawings from *Franz Schuster —Ein Möbelbuch. Ein Beitrag zum Problem des zeitgemässen Möbels* (Frankfurt am Main, 1932).
"From the basic elements of frame, box, drawer, and shelves you can put together almost any type of furniture you wish. The dimensions are 50, 100, and 150 cms. width." (From the brochure of the Erwin Behr Company: *Das Frankfurter Register, Aufbaumöbel von Franz Schuster.)*

24. Walter Gropius. Standard furniture. Designed in 1927 for Feder department store in Berlin, shown in 1930 at the Deutscher Werkbund Exhibition in Paris.
One of the great achievements of the Bauhaus was to seek contact with industry.

The simple, clear forms of this furniture not only conformed to the functional style of the late twenties but were easy to produce by industrial methods and were extremely durable.

25. Marcel Breuer. Club chair of steel tubing. 1926.
Industrial production was a way of bringing good and inexpensive furniture onto the market; Breuer worked out his first steel-chair designs with the aid of a metalworking firm in Berlin.

◁ 21, 22. Erich Mendelsohn. Einstein Tower, Potsdam. Exterior and interior views. 1919–20.
Architecture as sculpture; Expressionist thought in concrete form–typical of a time in which need was so great that it sometimes drove people to escape into utopias. The furniture in the shop with its stark, rectilinear shapes stands in opposition to the building's flowing lines.

25

26

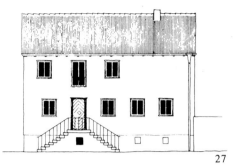

27

26. Werkbund Exhibition ''Die Wohn-ung,'' Weissenhof Project, Stuttgart. 1927. Overall planning by Mies van der Rohe.
This pioneering exhibition of the German Werkbund, with its presentation of modern home furnishings, sparked a discussion of rationalization and standardization in the field.

27. Paul Schmitthenner. Facade of a single-family house, Kochenhof Project, Stuttgart. 1933.
Conservative architecture began to come back into favor all over Europe in the early thirties. The style of these houses and the type of living they produced, typical of the post-1933 period, have continued to find many imitators throughout central Europe to this day.

28

29

the ruins of their civilization do not give much thought to aesthetic matters. Many more years were to pass before they had recovered from the shock and before the air of reaction had cleared.

America, however, had begun to make up for lost time. After years of stagnation, the ideas of great European architects—Mies van der Rohe, Walter Gropius, Marcel Breuer, and many others were now teaching at American universities—began to bear fruit on the new continent. They were supported in their endeavors by The Museum of Modern Art in New York, which as early as 1932 had organized the first large show of modern architecture there. In 1941 it sponsored a competition for modern furniture, which resulted in the now classic molded plywood chairs of Charles Eames and Eero Saarinen (Plate 31). Here for the first time the world began to see some of the peacetime results of the tremendous technical progress the United States had made during the war.

Companies like Knoll and Miller began to manufacture and distribute modern furniture by talented designers, and soon had reached a leading position on the international market. Their furniture by Mies van der Rohe, Marcel Breuer, Charles Eames, George Nelson, and Florence Knoll was a perfect complement to the interiors of the new skyscrapers of steel and glass that now began to go up everywhere.

In northern Europe the Bauhaus had prepared the ground well, and the crop began appearing in the late thirties. Firms like Artek in Finland—which worked with Alvar Aalto—and Hansen in Denmark pioneered a modern approach to furnituremaking which still left room for fine craftsmanship. The impeccable finish of their products was truly without compare, and it was no wonder that Scandinavian woodworking skill had soon won worldwide acclaim—especially in those parts of Europe that had suffered the most in the war, where what people wanted most in their homes was a feeling of warmth and security (Plates 33, 34). Denmark's Teak Style, with the help of farsighted trade policy and intelligent management, began to score its triumphs. In Sweden, the country that was soon to become the ideal of the welfare state, the government began an educational campaign to spread the principles of modern living among the population.

After the arduous work of reconstruction was over in Central Europe and affluence

30. Ludwig Mies van der Rohe. Tugendhat House, Brno. 1930.
The large and spacious living room, open on two sides to garden and conservatory, is articulated by freestanding walls and sparse furnishings.

◁ 28. P.L. Troost, L. Gall, and G. Troost. ''Haus der deutschen Kunst,'' Munich. 1936–37.
The Neoclassicism favored by Hitler made use of Roman and Greek elements, but with no consideration of human scale.

◁ 29. Albert Speer. ''Neue Reichskanzlei,'' Berlin. 1939. The Führer's study with a group of furniture around the fireplace.
Cumbrous and pseudo-aristocratic ensembles of this type survived the war and are still offered today in countless furniture catalogues.

began to grow, people began to turn back to a past that by now seemed almost classic. Art schools took up Bauhaus ideas and expanded on them, and it was not long until the furniture companies began to realize that there was money to be made in modern design—with a few changes here and there to suit the public taste. On the other hand, the world was growing steadily smaller as air travel became faster and cheaper, and tourists saw rustic furniture in Spain and Louis XV pieces in France. The result was a new eclecticism in Europe, that strange style of furniture that seems to have been based more than anything else on glossy magazine reports showing how the movie stars and top executives live. If the style of the tiny houses that now began to inundate the suburban landscape could be called pseudo-realistic, their furnishings were nothing if not pseudo-modern.

It was Italy—a country where people ''live in the streets'' and where social distinctions are among the crassest in Europe—that brought about a renaissance in home furnishings shortly after the war, largely thanks to the Milan school of designers and to experiments with the new material of plastic. Daring furniture companies, most of them quite small, had soon found out that this versatile product offered almost countless possibilities, and the cooperation between northern Italian business and progressive designers became a phenomenon much admired and envied all over Europe.

The combination of American technical expertise and Italian design originality led to a completely new type of furniture production on an international scale (Plates 35,

31

A3501

CONVERSATION

31. Charles Eames and Eero Saarinen. Design for an armchair. 1940. The Museum of Modern Art, New York.
This chair won one of the ten first prizes in the contest "Organic Design in Home Furnishings," sponsored by The Museum of Modern Art in 1941.

32. Ernest Flagg. Equitable Building, New York. 1915.
Skyscraper architecture in the United States was largely dependent on historical models until shortly before World War II.

36). The pressures of competition soon drove prices down on many models, and a diverse line of products for every budget was soon available. Of course the laws of the marketplace meant that new models had to be developed continually if production was to be maintained, and often enough quality suffered in the process. But as long as things were new and sensational enough, the average buyer did not seem to care.

The quiet clarity of Bauhaus interiors and the furniture designed for the housing projects of the twenties are not in much demand today. Life styles of the seventies require flexibility and variability in home furnishings, and the seemingly limitless possibilities of the "interior landscapes" on sale nowadays to adapt to changing

33. Hans J. Wegner. Armchair. 1949. Teak with wicker seat. Made by Johannes Hansen, Master Cabinetmaker.
Perfect craftsmanship and unerring choice of materials made Danish furniture world-famous after World War II.

patterns of family life are a good case in point (Plates 37, 38). Others prefer the trusty old furniture of yesteryear, bought cheaply at the flea market, or copies of Art Nouveau chairs, which, once the epitome of the craftsman's skill, are now being mass-produced.

Western industrial society shares the planet with two opposing worlds today. One is the Far East, which, though ostensibly an ideal to be emulated in social and political terms, is absolutely dependent on the West for design ideas, even supplying us with droves of cheap copies of old European furniture styles. As yet we have seen no truly independent furnishing ideas from that part of the world, not even in areas in which you would most expect it—in the design and furnishing of community centers, say.

Then there is the Third World, which also lives from Western ideas in the field of home furnishings. The sad fact is that traditional forms of living are fast being abandoned in favor of imported ideas, though they may have nothing in common with the customs and mores that have come down over the centuries. It appears that the dream of someday becoming an industrialized nation often overshadows every other consideration.

As we enter the last quarter of the twentieth century, there is one bright prospect on

34

34. Bard Henriksen. Renovated attic floor, eighteenth-century house in Copenhagen. The simple shapes of chairs by Arne Jacobsen give this room, which makes no pretense to unity or luxury, the atmosphere of comfortable, modern living.

the horizon. Young people seem to be interested in other things nowadays besides making money, and want to live in apartments that are furnished inexpensively and sensibly, with freedom to come and go as they please. Perhaps we may find a way after all to put some of William Morris's ideas into practice, and to bring about a truly social age—not by abolishing all machines, of course, but by using them to make those products we consider good and just, for an environment that expresses what it means to be human in today's world.

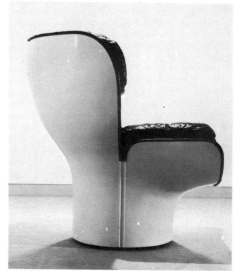

35. Joe C. Colombo. ''Elda 1005'' upholstered chair. 1965.
Manufactured by Comfort, Giorgetti Fratelli & Co.
The use of plastic—here combined with the traditional material, leather—was one of the most important steps in the development of furnituremaking after the Second World War.

36. Giancarlo Piretti. ''Plia'' folding chair. 1969. Manufactured by Anonima Castelli .
Space-saving, light, and inexpensive—the typical mass-produced chair for our time. The frame is aluminum; the seat and back, transparent plastic.

36

37

38

37. Walter Müller. ''Podium 3'' furniture system. 1972. Manufactured by Interlübke. Cabinets, shelves, and other units of many different kinds can be built up out of individual elements (dividers, drawers, and top plates) and held together by metal pins.

38. Rolf Heide. Terrace furniture. 1975. Manufactured by Wohnbedarf.
An easily assembled construction of wood with canvas covers, which can be used either indoors or out. Imagination and the use of simple materials, together with a high degree of variability that allows any number of possible uses, point the way to new ideas for living in our time.

Anonymous Furniture in the Nineteenth Century—
Harbingers of the Machine Aesthetic

Most of the nineteenth-century furniture that proved germinal to modern design was in its own day anonymous and marginal. Only by hindsight do the light Chiavari chairs, the graceful iron benches once fashionable in England and France, or the furniture made by religious communities like the Shakers in America seem significant and rich in associations; they were made to be used, and no one thought of them in terms of design or style. Not even the pioneers of modern architecture realized how well many of these pieces complemented their own interiors until the 1920s and the thirties—the one exception being the bentwood chair invented by Michael Thonet. Thonet's new process fascinated Adolf Loos and Josef Hoffmann as early as 1900, and Otto Wagner ordered office furniture for his Post Office Savings Bank (1904–6, extended 1910–12) from Thonet's Vienna factories. Also, it is hard to imagine Le Corbusier's first domestic interiors and exhibition pavilions without the "Viennese Chairs" that formed such an integral part of them (Plate 97).

This is perhaps a good place to mention a type of wooden furniture that has been manufactured for centuries according to almost unchanged patterns (Plates 39, 40). These simple chairs, made of wood from local forests with seats woven of local straw, still grace countless Italian trattorias, Spanish bodegas, and country inns all over Europe today—not to mention converted farmhouses whose new owners want to furnish them in a suitably rustic style. Another and perhaps better reason for their popularity is their inexpensiveness and durability, combined with formal qualities that appeal to our contemporary taste for unpretentious, practical furniture.

The new industries of the nineteenth century not only provided new materials in great quantity to the furnituremaking art, they also faced it with new problems. Tractor seats had to be designed, for instance, or fittings for railroad cars, or office furniture. There was a widespread incentive to improve working conditions for growing sectors of the population, such as office workers, and to make living in general more comfortable. The dawn of the mass age forced fledgling industry to experiment; it is no wonder that the first results were not always completely satisfying.

Though division of labor was not unknown before the advent of the Industrial Revolution, as we look back it is very difficult to draw a clear dividing line between handicrafts and mercantile manufacture, early industrial production and mass production. This is particularly true in the case of furnituremaking. Furniture is not only a part of the world of objects we use unthinkingly every day; it is an expression of man's domestic drive and even of his inmost, unconscious wishes. The diversity of needs furniture must fulfill cannot in the end, it seems, be satisfied by large-scale mass production alone. Even in the present day the manufacture of a chair or table may still be determined by considerations that run the gamut from the purely aesthetic at the one end to the strictly and aridly functional at the other.

The history of style in the nineteenth century is marked by historical revivals. The new social strata that arose in Europe in the wake of the French Revolution—a new bourgeoisie, headed by prosperous entrepreneurs—still followed the aristocracy in

39. French ladder chair. Nineteenth century. Poplar with rush seat. Die Neue Sammlung, Munich.
In rural areas simple, artisan-made furniture has often held its own for centuries.

40. Vincent van Gogh. *Bedroom at Arles.* 1889. Stedelijk Museum, Van Gogh Bequest, Amsterdam.
The furnishings of this room could not be simpler. Furniture and fixtures were made in small workshops which retained their methods and designs unchanged for decades.

matters of taste. Conservative styles in furniture began to oust Empire and Biedermeier; public authorities, if anything, encouraged the stylistic anarchy that ensued, while such theoreticians of an architecture to come as Eugène-Emmanuel Viollet-le-Duc (1814–79) and Gottfried Semper (1803–79) attempted to direct the chaos into narrower and purer channels. With the introduction of new machines and methods, the production of historically inspired furniture began to burgeon. Greater demand on the part of a growing buying public only increased competition on the marketplace; fashions were created only to be replaced by new ones, and the first signs of what we would today call planned obsolescence began to appear. As demand rose, taste declined. Yet if it had not been for the Historical Revival and the continual training in orthodox furnituremaking it gave to manufacturers, they would have been in no position to cope with the tasks set them later by the architects of Art Nouveau or a man like Adolf Loos. A good illustration of this is Loos's obituary for the old cabinetmaker, Veillich:

They buried him yesterday. Veillich made all my dining-room chairs. He was my faithful collaborator for thirty years. Up to the war he employed an assistant, whose work he valued highly. He didn't have much good to say about people nowadays. His assistant was killed in the war. He worked alone ever since. He did not want to make worse chairs than before; they would have been too expensive anyway. And in the end there was not enough work even for him to do. My students abroad kept him busy. As a young man he had worked in Paris. He was deaf, like me; that's why we understood each other so well. How he selected the wood for each type of chair! He used boards from the lower part of the trunk for the back legs, and the annual rings of the wood had to follow their curve exactly. And—but no, why should I reveal the secrets of a workshop that has died?[1]

Iron Furniture

In the eighteenth century and at the beginning of the nineteenth ... the technique of the non-English countries was still so backward that a general history of iron need only report of these countries when and where English methods were introduced. (Otto Johannsen)[2]

Iron, a material long known to other fields, did not find its way into furnituremaking until a smelting process was invented that lowered its cost considerably. The spiritual fathers of the almost indestructible but very cumbersome cast-iron furniture that ensued were industrialists who, with a certain cultural naïveté, tried to adapt traditional styles to their new materials and production methods. Even the designers many of them employed worked in one or another of the fashionable historical styles. From a purely technical point of view, there was no problem involved in turning out intricate Victorian ornament more cheaply in iron than in wood (and painting it to look like the latter). Basically, the cast-iron furniture that was to be found in so many country houses of the period was only a byproduct of the manufacture of iron stoves and grates, particularly by English firms. One of the largest and best of these was the Coalbrookdale Company; garden benches very similar to theirs (Plate 48) can still be seen in the malls of shopping centers in the suburbs of Stockholm.

42. Group of officers in the Sacher Garden ▷ of the Vienna Prater. c. 1900.
These chairs, made of thin iron rod, are clearly related to Thonet chairs of bentwood (see also the chair on the left in Plate 12). The shape of the back may also be traced to Thonet Chair No. 1 (see Plate 75).

43. French garden chair. Last half of the ▷ nineteenth century. Iron. Die Neue Sammlung, Munich.
A formal solution suggested by the properties of the material and necessities of construction; the seat is made of perforated sheet iron. The shape of the armrests is very close to that of early Thonet armchairs.

41. Édouard Manet. *Concert in the Tuileries*. c. 1860. National Gallery, London.
This painting of about mid-century shows the type of chair that was then in general use in public parks and still can be found in the Tuileries in Paris today.

41

42

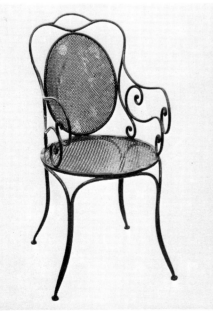

Toward the end of the nineteenth century the demand for cast-iron furniture began to decline, and many factories closed down. Their products lasted much too long, and iron as a material had lost its novelty. Even more important, perhaps, were demands for the renewal of metalworking as a craft along medieval lines, formulated by men such as A.W.N. Pugin, a vehement propagandizer for neo-Gothic architecture, and William Morris. In any case, industrial cast iron had to give way to the more "authentic" wrought iron, with its completely different methods of production. Its high cost limited its application, however, and wrought-iron furniture reached only very small numbers of people.

Many factories continued to produce furniture by both methods, often in combination with thin spring steel. The page illustrated from the catalogue of the Société Anonyme des Hauts-Fourneaux & Fonderies du Val d'Osne (Plate 45), which had its main offices in Paris, shows some of the results. The simple and very popular garden chairs made of welded iron rod (Plates 42, 43) that are often so reminiscent of Thonet designs (and often found their way into Impressionist paintings—see Plate 41) perhaps appeal most to modern sensibilities. They certainly did to Le Corbusier.

Another interesting product of the last century is metal beds, probably developed

43

for reasons of hygiene (Plate 46). They were turned out in great numbers—a Birmingham factory was making 6000 bedsteads of brass and iron a week in 1875, most of which were for export. And iron rocking chairs of unusually clean design appeared on the market as early as the Great Exhibition of 1851 in London (Plate 49).

Steel tube does not seem to have been used for furniture to any significant extent at this time, though Gandillot in France made some chairs in 1844 out of the kind of pipe used for plumbing and gas lines; unfortunately, he painted them to look like wood. The bicycle manufacturer William Starley (1858–1937) of Coventry appears to have been the first to experiment with steel tubing for furniture. Starley, who held many patents on his inventions, brought home some newfangled steel office chairs with him one day to show to his family—their protests, however, led him to give up all further work along these lines.

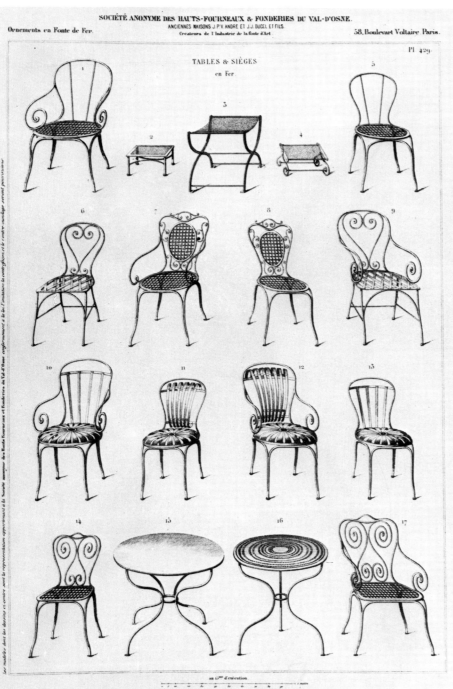

45

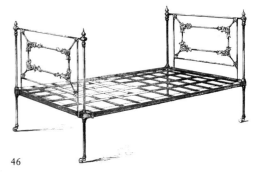

44. Luigi Elli. Theater seats. Iron frames and cane or upholstered seats. Museo Poldi-Pezzoli, Milan.
Both the use of iron and bentwood for theater seating (in 1888 the first folding chairs were installed at the Deutsches Volkstheater in Vienna) led to constructions that brought great space savings.

45. Catalogue page of the Société Anonyme des Hauts-Fourneaux & Fonderies du Val d'Osne. c. 1870.
The opening of the parks to the public in the big cities of Europe went hand in hand with the mass production of light iron furniture.

46. Cowley & James, Walsall. Brass bed. Shown at the Great Exhibition in London, 1851.
The technical capabilities of metal casting allowed designers to borrow shapes from earlier furniture and architecture and apply them to a new material.

47

47. Chair and stool of cast iron. c. 1840. Modern copy of a cast by the Fonderies du Val d'Osne. Musée des Arts Décoratifs, Paris.

48

48. Garden bench of cast iron, with fern motif on backrest. 1850. From the catalogue of the Coalbrookdale Company.
Abraham I. Darley succeeded in firing a blast furnace with coke in 1709. He leased an abandoned iron works in Coalbrookdale, Shropshire, with the resulting company specializing in the cast-iron garden furniture so popular during the Victorian Age.

49. English rocking chair of cast iron, with velvet upholstery. c. 1850. Die Neue Sammlung, Munich.
This extremely elegant rocking chair, if not already on show in 1851 in the Crystal Palace, definitely was in 1862 at the International Exhibition.

49

The Mechanization of Furniture

In his book *Mechanization Takes Command*,[3] Sigfried Giedion, whose influence on contemporary American furniture design would be hard to overestimate, dealt in detail with the development of mechanical furniture in the nineteenth century. As early as 1850, he recounts, mechanical appliances were already in use in many American households, and their anonymous inventors had already begun to apply their skills to the mechanization of furniture, particularly chairs for special tasks. Working hand in hand with industry they developed barber chairs (Plate 54), which were also used by doctors and dentists for simple operations, and appointments for railroad sleeping and dining cars (Plate 57), for which they often found technically brilliant solutions. American office furniture, developed to save space and labor in the first large-scale offices introduced about 1890, was also far ahead of its time. After that, these pioneering inventions seem to have dropped out of sight for decades. It was not until after World War II that the perfectly mechanized office systems we take for granted today appeared on the market, forging a link with the past.

Writing in *Nineteenth Century English Furniture*,[4] Elizabeth Aslin lists some of the countless inventions shown during the heyday of the great world exhibitions. Though it did not appear in the illustrated catalogue, mechanical furniture had already made its debut at one of the first of these, the Great Exhibition of 1851 held in London. These mechanized wheelchairs, compact ship's furniture, and convertible furnishings of an incredible number of different kinds are eloquent testimony, in the heartland of industry as elsewhere in Europe, to the inventive spirit of the nineteenth century.

What makes mechanized furniture so interesting for us today is its variability and convertibility, two modern principles that its designers put to the test for the first time. The need to solve certain problems that went along with technical progress, such as how best to use the limited space in Pullman cars, eventually led them to solutions that were so new that they in turn brought about changes in social mores—people riding in a Pullman car, it is safe to say, found it very difficult to

50. Wheelchair. c. 1830. Bundessammlung alter Stilmöbel, Vienna.
Mechanized furniture for special purposes appeared very early in furniture history. In 1780 Benjamin Franklin designed a chair for his library which could be transformed into a stepladder. The invalids' wheelchair illustrated here—it is equipped with a collapsible sunshade or screen—was built for Kaiser Franz I of Austria.

51. Dining table and chairs, after a United States patent of 1889.
The flexible connection between chairs and table was meant to make dining on rough seas easier.

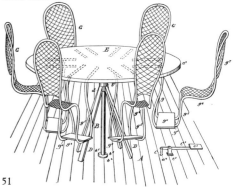

51

52. G. Wilson. Drawing of folding chair of iron, after a United States patent of 1871.

53. G. Wilson. Folding chair of iron, after a United States patent of 1871.
By pressing a lever the user can put this chair into almost every conceivable position without having to get up.

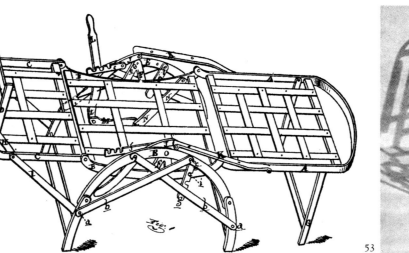

52

53

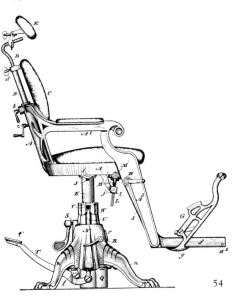

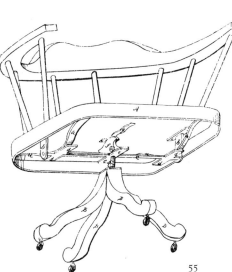

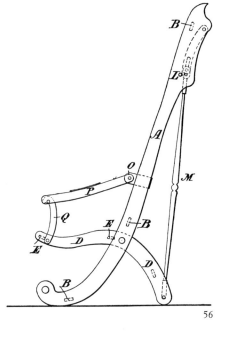

54

55

56

57

54. Dentist chair, after a United States patent of 1879.
By the mid-nineteenth century in America, adjustable barber chairs had already been developed to facilitate not only haircutting, but such operations as toothpulling and bloodletting. By 1860 the patent office had begun to differentiate between barber and dentist chairs, the latter having become technically much more complex. Hydraulic cylinders to raise and lower the seat had come in by 1880.

55. Chair, after a United States patent of 1853.
Originally to be found only in the parlor, this "sitting chair," as its inventor called it, was later widely used in offices. Its construction allows the seat to be turned and tilted.

56. Armchair, after a United States patent of 1874.
When tilted 90 degrees backwards this chair becomes a couch, the seat becoming the backrest.

57. George M. Pullman. Dining car, after a United States patent of 1869.
The great distances in America made it necessary to develop comfortable train furnishings which, in contrast to Europe, were not divided into classes, with the exception of a separate class for Negroes. The best of them were invented during the heyday of patent furniture. Here are two of Pullman's patents: above, the hotel car, in which passengers (and particularly families) could travel, eat, and sleep; below, the dining car, without sleeping facilities.

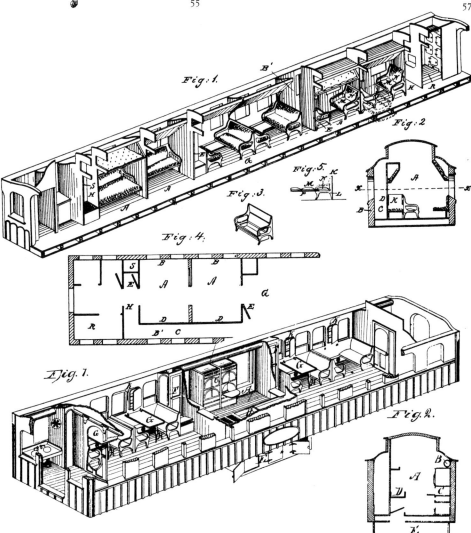

58

practice Victorian etiquette. The influences of multi-functional furniture on modern home furnishing ideas are too numerous to list—convertible sofa beds designed to save space in tiny modern apartments are a case in point.

Chiavari's ''Campanino''—or, How to Improve on a Traditional Form

The grace of the chairs made in the Chiavari workshops near Genoa is the result of a long series of logical changes in a given form. The story runs as follows: a certain Marchese Stefano Rivarola brought a light chair from Paris in 1807 and gave it to Gaetano Descalzi (1767–1855), a cabinetmaker nicknamed ''Campanino,'' to copy. This he did. When the resulting chair was shown to Antonio Canova, the famous Neoclassic sculptor, he exclaimed, ''The problem of how to combine the greatest lightness with the greatest strength has been solved.''

This chair became known simply as ''Campanino'' or ''Leggero'' (Plates 58, 60). Its maker reduced its construction to the simplest terms, fitting the frame together with straightforward joints and weaving the seat by what was then a new process—willow slips braided together into herringbone or checkerboard patterns. Decisive for the chair's success, aside from its lightness and comfort, was the fact that Campanino did not use expensive, imported woods in its manufacture, but wood from the forests around Chiavari—cherry, walnut, and particularly maple, whose

58. J.S. van den Abeele. *Salon of Villa Paolina with Zenaide Bonaparte and Her Children.* c. 1840. Watercolor. Museo Napoleonico, Primoli, Rome.
Classicistic decor and furnishings from the late Empire period stand in contrast to the extremely light and elegant Chiavari chairs.

60. Giovanni Battista Ravenna. Chair. c. ▷ 1825. Fruitwood with woven seat.
Chair in the Chiavari manner with comfortable backrest (see also Plate 58). On many of the Chiavari designs the round back legs, like those of bentwood chairs, continued on in one piece into the back. The density of the woven seat depended on the quality; Canepa succeeded in weaving up to 22 willow slips per square centimeter, the groups of slips being called ''costane.'' The better chairs had up to 65 ''costane'' per seat, the least expensive seven, arranged in either a herringbone or checkerboard pattern.

59. Emanuele Rambaldi. Chair. c. 1933. Maple with woven seat and back.
This chair, made at Chiavari, was clearly influenced by the Bauhaus and the chairs of steel tubing developed there.

light color lent the chair its characteristic elegance. The method of its manufacture was specialized in the simplest sense of the term: Campanino trained local peasants to do the rough cutting of the pieces. G.B. Canepa, Campanino's son-in-law, "modernized" the simple shape of the Chiavari chair in the mid-nineteenth century to conform to the fashion for neo-Gothic and other historical styles (Plate 61).

Initially, Campanino and his sons, with 50 workers, turned out about 5000 chairs a year. By 1870 his Chiavari workshops employed about 150 trained workmen and 60 peasants to produce 25,000 chairs annually at a price of about seven *lire* each. In 1844 a branch had been established at Trieste, at that time still part of the Austro-Hungarian Empire, to help fill the many orders that began coming in from abroad—among others from Napoleon III and Metternich, the man who brought Michael Thonet to Vienna.

In our own century—about 1933, to be exact—the young modern-design movement in Italy turned the experience and expertise of the Chiavari craftsmen to its own use. In the chair designed by one of its members, Emanuele Rambaldi (Plate 59), a certain austerity has taken the place of the elegance of the original form, probably under Bauhaus influence. After World War II, Italian architects again revived the simple chair, which fitted perfectly into the ascetic interiors of the period. In 1952 and 1957, Gio Ponti designed several models (Plate 62) which owe a great debt to the "Leggero." Their timeless forms, thought through with care and simplified to the last detail, hold their own even in such extremely personal interiors as those designed

59

60

61. Lathe-turned chair from Chiavari. c. 1860. Meroni Collection, Porana.
The influence of Historicism began to make itself felt even in Chiavari chairs about the middle of the century, and they lost their graceful lightness.

62. Gio Ponti. Chair. 1952. Ash. Manufactured by Cassina.
Ponti designed chairs for the Cassina firm in the 1950s that were quite on a par with Chiavari chairs in terms of formal authority and grace. They are still being made today.

by the Milan school between 1950 and 1960. Here we see an ideal example of the way the old can complement the new—as bentwood chairs complement the interiors of our own day.

Anonymous Wicker Furniture

Like woodworking, basketweaving is one of the oldest skills practiced by man. For centuries the only means of transporting goods in many countries, baskets inspired early craftsmen to apply the idea to furniture—wicker chairs may be seen, for example, in ancient Chinese woodcuts and on Roman stone reliefs (Plate 63). In the nineteenth century in Germany, in Oberfranken near Coburg, a new branch of the basketweaving trade was established about 1896 to produce wicker furniture, probably inspired by the models on show at the Chicago Exhibition of 1893.

At about the same time the typical material used for this purpose, European willow or *Salix,* began to be supplemented by rattan imported from Indonesia and Malaysia. Both the core of the rattan stalk, which consists of a bundle of porous fibers, and the hard stalk itself, are cut and prepared in a number of different ways to serve various tasks. Their lightness and durability make wicker chairs ideal for use outdoors and in restaurants, particularly in hot and humid climates. Although their beautiful organic shapes must be produced largely by hand and in small numbers—machines can be used only for the preparatory steps—this very fact lends them a personal quality to be found in no other type of furniture. It also means, of course, that basket chairs can be easily produced in countries which have no highly developed industry.

The pioneers of modern architecture were not long in discovering wicker furniture—Adolf Loos used it often, for example in his Knižé menswear store in Paris, and Le Corbusier used it to furnish his early houses.

63. Toilet scene on a Roman sepulcher, found in Neumagen an der Mosel. c. 235. Rheinisches Landesmuseum, Trier.
The stonecutting work gives a clear picture of the geometric motifs on the basket chair. Baskets (probably for the storage and transport of grain), with an estimated age of 5000 to 7000 years, have been found near the coast of Syria. Two chairs made of cane and woven papyrus stalks from Tutankhamen's grave (c. 1340 B.C.) are an early example of the use of this material for furniture.

64

65

66. Nanna Ditzel. Chair and stool of Spanish cane. 1961. Manufactured by R. Wengler, Copenhagen.

67. Egon Eiremann. Basket chair of Spanish cane. 1952. Manufactured by Heinrich Murmann, Johannisthal bei Kronach, Bavaria.

68. Living room with wicker furniture in an American home. Architect W. C. Jones. Wicker furniture can be made either in rectilinear or free forms, its framework left open or filled in. The great rise in popularity it has seen in the past few years surely has much to do with its reasonable price; wages are low in the Third World countries where it is made, and raw material is locally available and cheap. Made according to European designs in East Asia (Hong Kong, for instance), these models arrive on the European market at low prices despite their very high shipping volume.

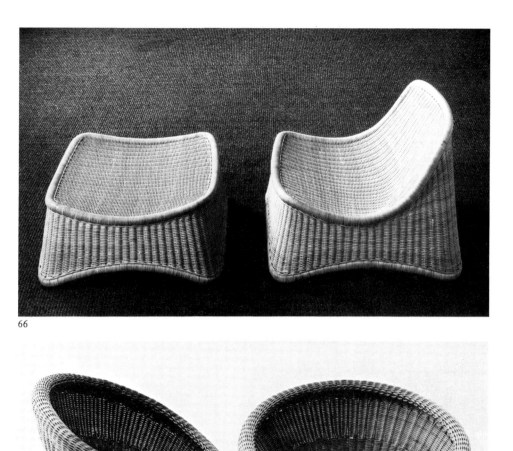

66

67

◁ 64. Exhibition opening, Weimar, 1904. (Third from the right, Henri van de Velde.) At the urging of Harry Graf Kessler, Henri van de Velde was called to Weimar as artistic adviser in 1901 by Grossherzog Wilhelm Ernst von Sachsen-Weimar. In the course of an arts-and-crafts seminar (which can be seen as the predecessor of the School of Applied Art), he designed products for Saxony's underdeveloped and ailing cottage industry, particularly for basketweaving, pottery, and toymaking. Art Nouveau wicker furniture was easier and cheaper to manufacture than comparable wooden models.

◁ 65. Wicker chair. c. 1930. State School of Basketmaking, Lichtenfels am Main. Materials for the frames of wicker furniture (palm cane, Calamus rattan) are Manila cane, the finest variety and lightest in color; Malacca cane, brownish in color inside and red-brown outside; and Manau cane, which comes in diameters up to 6 cms.

68

Michael Thonet and Bentwood Furniture

Michael Thonet (1796–1871) came from a line of craftsmen. In 1819 he opened a cabinetmaker's shop in the little town of Boppard on the Rhine. (David Roentgen, the great cabinetmaker and *ébéniste* of the eighteenth century, had had his workshop in nearby Neuwied, with one hundred journeymen—cabinetmakers, locksmiths, mechanics, and bronze founders already working on a division-of-labor basis.) About 1830 Thonet began to experiment with wood bending as a way of making some of the parts of his Biedermeier style of furniture. He began with chair backs and rungs, gluing strips of heavy veneer together and clamping them in forms made of wood; as time went by he solved more and more difficult problems, technical improvement going hand in hand with a simplification of form and reduction in the thickness of the parts. The light and elegant chairs he designed around 1840 (Plate 69) were such a success that Metternich recommended him to the Court at Vienna and got commissions for him from wealthy princely houses (such as Liechtenstein and Schwarzenberg, Plates 72, 75), which assured him of a living.

Thonet's furnishings for Palais Liechtenstein in Vienna (1843–46) include chair types that in their delicacy and purity of form are among the most beautiful examples of the furnituremaking art the nineteenth century produced (Plate 72). The firm of Carl Leistler, for whom Thonet worked when furnishing the Liechtenstein house (his are the parquet floors with beautiful curved shapes in bent wood), was quite famous at the time for its furniture (Plate 73). A comparison with Thonet's work makes the difference in their approach and technical skill abundantly clear.

Thonet established his own workshop in Vienna in 1849. The same year, Café Daum became the first in a long line of coffeehouses (Plates 95, 98) to be furnished with Thonet Chair No. 4 in mahogany (Plates 76, 77). In the chairs designed for the Great Exhibition of 1851 (Plate 74) we already see the shapes of mass-produced goods to come—the triangular connection between the front legs and seat frame, for instance, can be found in many of the later, industrially made models, up to about 1875 (e.g., No. 13, Plate 79). From these "luxury chairs" developed, little by little, those models whose successful sales enabled Thonet to begin working on an industrial basis.

The way in which Thonet went about building his first factory in Koritschan (Moravia) earns him the title of a pioneer of industry. He drew up the plans himself, supervised the construction of the building and the equipment, and, together with his five sons, even designed a great deal of the machinery himself. The factory was opened in 1856. The area in which it was built had the advantage of cheap, rural labor and large tracts of red-beech woods—a variety of wood which later was to become central to the production of bentwood furniture.

71. Page from the Thonet Brothers' catalogue. c. 1873.
This page shows the development of the early Thonet chairs from No. 1 to No. 21, as well as the rocking chair and a few of their special models (office chairs, children's furniture). The simple forms were given a more ornamental touch on benches or tables, a very good demonstration of the many possibilities inherent in the bentwood process.

69. Michael Thonet. Armchair. c. 1840.
In early Thonet models, which of course were made entirely by hand, we see new technical processes coupled with traditional, late Biedermeier forms. Delicate dimensioning (particularly of the legs) lends this chair its lightness and elegance.

69

70

70. Bending wood in a Thonet factory. c. 1900.
"The material, cut into laths, is rendered flexible by subjecting it to hot water vapor for a few minutes (steaming), then the steamed laths are stretched over iron forms (bending) and allowed to dry in that position, and finally they are brought into final shape by mechanical means. Lightness, strength, elasticity, and great durability are the main qualities of furniture made of bentwood. Their main parts are connected to each other by bolts only—there is no glue used whatsoever."[5]

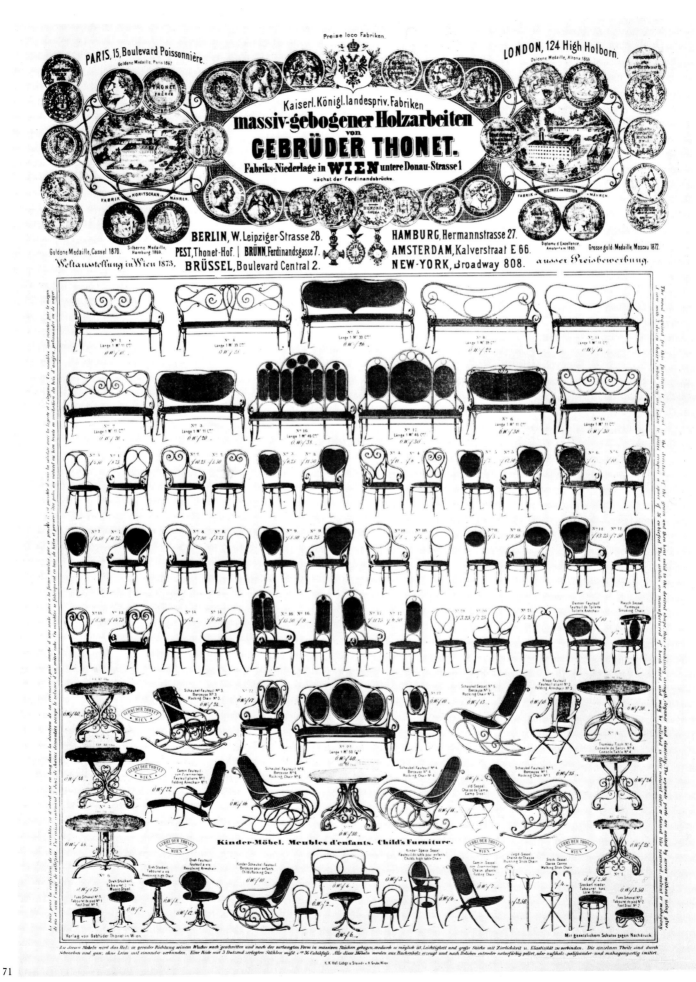

72

73

72. Michael Thonet. Three upholstered
chairs in bentwood technique and parquet
floors for Palais Liechtenstein, Vienna. c.
1845.

The chair on the left is gold-plated. Here
Thonet has taken the bentwood process to
the peak of refinement as a craft, as can be
seen in the length of the parts used and the
way the transition between seat and chair
legs is handled. Cutting the pieces for this
parquet floor (they were shaped by steaming
beforehand) was Thonet's first assignment
in Vienna.

73. Carl Leistler. Upholstered chair. c.
1845. Palais Liechtenstein, Vienna.

The interior design of a number of rooms of
the Palais Liechtenstein, carried out by the
firm of Carl Leistler (for whom Thonet
worked at that time) according to designs by
the English architect P.M. Devignes, must
be considered masterpieces of Second
Rococo in Vienna. The chairs were made by
traditional methods—carved of solid wood
by craftsmen.

74. Michael Thonet. Chair, armchair,
bench, and table of rosewood; and table with
brass inlays. For the Great Exhibition in
London, 1851.

Thonet wanted to show "luxury furniture"
at the Crystal Palace, so he pulled all the
stops of his bentwood technique to produce
such rich orchestrations as these table
frames, for instance. The much simpler
chairs, by contrast, already have the shapes
that were soon to go into mass production.

74

75

76

77

78

79

80

75. Thonet Chair No. 1 (early version). Palais Schwarzenberg, Vienna.

76. Thonet Chair No. 4 (early version).

77. Thonet Chair No. 4 (version with leg ring and reinforcement of the back legs). Technisches Museum für Industrie und Gewerbe, Vienna.

78. Thonet Chair No. 6.

79. Thonet Chair No. 13.

80. Thonet Chair No. 16.

Chairs No. 6 and 13 are no longer to be found in the Thonet catalogue of 1911.

Progressively greater mechanization of manufacture could no longer deal with the complex shapes of their backs.

As early as 1849 Chair No. 4 was already being made in mahogany for Café Daum in Vienna.

Chairs No. 16 and 17 (see also catalogue page, Plate 71), the only ones in the entire line with high backs, can probably be traced to the influence of English furniture. Thonet has begun making No. 17 again recently, and general nostalgia has made it a great sales success.

81   82

83

Many of the chairs that Thonet exported to South America were damaged by the humid climate, so it was decided to discontinue the use of laminated parts. The logical solution was to make them of solid wood, but this caused great difficulties at first, since the parts splintered at points of tension. It was not until Thonet hit on the idea of using steel inlays and screwing or bolting the wooden elements to them that the problem was solved—now, nothing more stood in the way of full mass production. In 1859, at the peak of the Historical Revival, Thonet brought out a model beyond which no further simplification seemed possible (Chair No. 14, Plate 86; the numbers quoted are those of the old Thonet catalogue). The *Konsumsessel,* or consumers' chair, was born.

The chair was supplied in kit form, to be assembled at its destination. It was light and durable; could be used almost anywhere, indoors and out; and if the joints started

81. Thonet Chair No. 18. Since 1867.
82. Thonet Chair No. 56. Since 1885.
83. Thonet Chair No. 221. Since 1898.

After the No. 14 series (Plate 86), Chairs No. 18, 56, and 221 are the largest selling in Thonet's line. Chair No. 18, robust and easy to assemble, has turned out to be *the* export model.

A decisive change was made beginning with No. 50: Thonet began making the back legs separately from the backrest. This simplified the bending process, which still involved a lot of handwork, by shortening the parts from a little over two to less than one meter in length.

Chair No. 56 has reinforcements at the upper end of the back legs, probably to ensure a strong enough joint with the shortened backrest. Series No. 56 and 221 have become the café chairs par excellence; the backrest of the latter is more in accord with modern design ideas, in addition to being much more comfortable.

84. Chair, "woven" of three lengths of wood. Technisches Museum für Industrie und Gewerbe, Vienna.

An exhibition piece made to demonstrate the technical possibilities of the bentwood process.

85. Thonet chair, made of one continuous piece of molded wood. c. 1870.

Only a few examples of this chair, which was probably made for experimental purposes and was not listed in the catalogue,

84   85

survive today in museums. Similar methods were used sixty years later to mold the heavy laminated elements of Alvar Aalto's chairs.

86. Thonet Chair No. 14. Since 1859. By 1930 over 50 million of this "classic" model had been produced, and it is still being made today.

87, 88. Tools for bending backrests and seat frames. Technisches Museum für Industrie und Gewerbe, Vienna.
"The most significant phase in the history of this industry began. Thonet utilized the following method: on that surface of the as yet unbent wooden rod which was to form the convex surface after bending, an iron strip was laid and fastened to it with C-clamps at several spots and at both ends so that it could not move. Now, when the rod was bent, the part of the wood fastened to the iron strip could not stretch more than the strip itself, in other words by an insignificant amount. In order to bend at all, then, the entire piece of wood had to compress, the fibers farthest away from the iron strip, i.e. closest to the concave side, having to compress the most. The natural law governing the position of the neutral layer was put out of force, and the neutral layer transferred to the convex surface. Furthermore, there was no longer a lengthening of one side of the rod and a compression of the other; the strip of iron, fastened immovably to the rod, forced *all* the fibers of the wood closer together" (Wilhelm Franz Exner).[6]

86

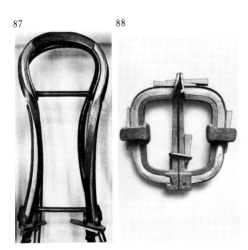

87　　88

to wobble, all you had to do was tighten the screws. Ease of transport and excellent distribution all over the world made the Thonet Company a rapidly growing enterprise, and it soon began to establish branch offices, lease sawmills, and build its own railway lines.

Tradition has it that it was August Thonet, one of Michael Thonet's five sons, who developed most of the new types of chair with the aid of a few assistants. Whoever designed them, there can be no doubt that many of the most popular—No. 3, No. 9, a desk chair, and No. 1, a rocking chair—have a quiet elegance combined with practical utility that has made them classics of modern furnituremaking art.

In 1869 the company's first patents expired, opening the market for competitors. Michael Thonet died two years later. The catalogue page illustrated here (Plate 71), probably dating from the Vienna World Exhibition of 1873, suggests that it was he who had kept the forms of the entire line of furniture so pure. The problem of obtaining good, knot-free wood was finally solved, after several unsuccessful attempts, with the introduction of Chair No. 56 (Plate 82)—the length of material needed for its back legs was only half that of the continuous back of earlier models. Chair No. 221, another new type, combines a more comfortable backrest with forms that may well have been inspired by late Rococo (Plate 83). This chair and those to follow lent the Viennese café of the *fin de siècle* its inimitable atmosphere.

A number of the very interesting experiments made at that time cannot be dated with any precision, such as the chair "woven" of only three lengths of wood, apparently meant as an exhibition piece (Plate 84). Even more important in terms of future developments was plywood furniture (Plate 85). It apparently never got beyond the experimental stage, however, and was not produced in very great numbers.

Thonet catalogues from the turn of the century illustrate furniture of every imaginable kind (Plates 90–94), including armchairs and settees for bedrooms, for outdoor use, and even scaled-down versions for children. Their designs often stood in crass contrast to "classic" models such as No. 14 (Plate 86). Historicism made its incursions, if belatedly, even here, but in addition to the overloaded Makart-style productions the models that embodied Michael Thonet's pioneer spirit continued to be offered. The two great pathfinders of modern architecture, Adolf Loos and Le Corbusier (Plate 97), used Thonet mass-produced furniture and realized its importance. Otto Wagner's chairs for his Post Office Savings Bank in Vienna (Plate 96) were made partly by Thonet and partly by Kohn & Kohn, their competitor, and Josef Hoffmann and his followers in the Vienna School did not tire of experimenting with the possibilities of the bentwood technique. In the last third of the nineteenth century true mass production got under way at Thonet. In 1876, for example, 4500 workers, 10 steam engines, and 280 horses turned out 2000 pieces of bentwood furniture a day, 1750 of which were chairs, and by 1900 the daily production of the twenty-six branches of the factory had risen to 15,000 pieces—a boom that was unprecedented even in those days of rampant industrialism.

Michael Thonet's central achievement, however, remains his classic Chair No. 14. It was as much at home in fine salons as in genteel drawing rooms or coffeehouses. William Morris and Henri van de Velde may have talked Socialism, but their clients were kings, aristocrats, and bankers. Thonet, helped onto his feet by the aristocratic elite of old Austria, produced *the* chair for millions. Honesty of

89

89. Ferdinand Fellner, Jr. The Thonet House on Stephansplatz (corner of Rotenturmstrasse), Vienna. 1875–76 (destroyed). The Thonet House, which was destroyed in the last few days of the war in 1945, shows that the management of the company, when it was not a matter of bentwood chairs, was by no means immune to the prevailing Historicist style.

90

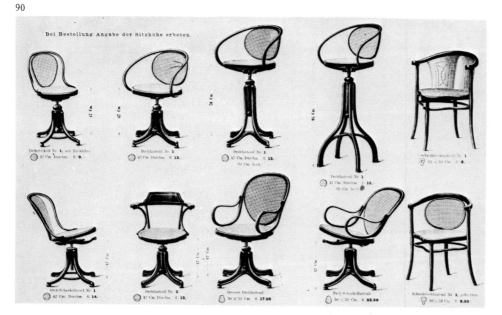

90. Office furniture, Thonet catalogue of 1911 and 1915 supplement. Catalogue descriptions: revolving chair (top row, left); revolving fauteuil (top row, middle); revolving rocking fauteuil (bottom row, second from right).
In these office chairs we see a very early and happy connection (some of them were already illustrated on the catalogue page shown in Plate 71) between technical progress and aesthetically satisfying design.

93. Thonet Wardrobe No. 10.907a (known ▷ as a wall clothes rack).

94. Thonet Rocking Chair No. 7027. ▷ Thonet began manufacturing rocking chairs in 1860, and soon was turning out over 100,000 a year.

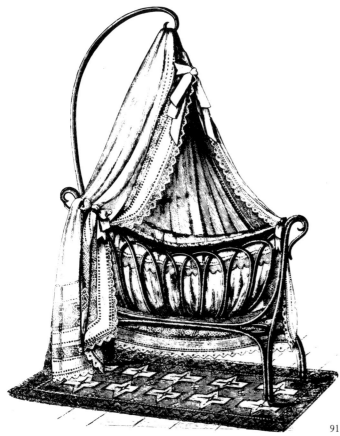

91. Child's cradle, Thonet catalogue.

92. Desk Chair No. 6009 (later Thonet-Mundus B 9). Model with pokerwork design This more than any other Thonet model is the embodiment of the ''Viennese chair,'' as bentwood furniture is still known in northern Europe. Le Corbusier and Alvar Aalto used it in the twenties.

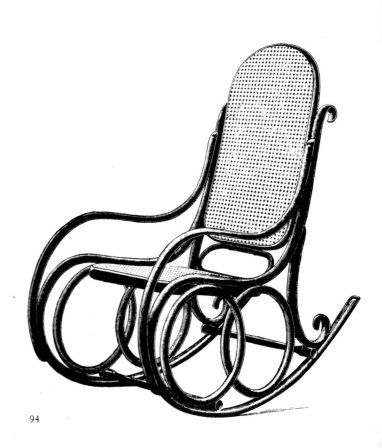

93   94

95

95. Rudolf Völkel. *Das Literaten-Café Griensteidl*. c. 1885. Detail of a watercolor. Vienna's famous writers' café—opened in 1847 on the ground-floor premises of Palais Herberstein on Herrengasse and refurbished in 1856—was famed just as much for its luxurious furnishings as for the countless newspapers in all languages provided for the use of its clientele. It was a must for young writers and actors to be seen at Griensteidl, one of the many Viennese coffeehouses to be furnished with Thonet chairs.

96. Otto Wagner. Seating for the Post Office Savings Bank, Vienna. 1904–6.
The stools in the main waiting room, the armchairs for the conference room (one of which can be seen in the left background), and the upholstered chairs for the executive offices are all still in use today. Wagner replaced the usual round-sectioned bentwood by rectangular parts and used new materials, such as aluminum, for the feet and straps of the armchairs.
The stools, despite their innovative form, were constructed by traditional bentwood technique and the individual parts bolted together.

96

construction and fitness of materials had led, already in 1860, to an anonymous product that fulfilled all the demands of beginning mass consumption. With Michael Thonet's achievement two significant components of the age of the Industrial Revolution—pioneering spirit applied to technology and the fulfillment of the demands of a new class—entered such an early and happy marriage that we are justified in speaking of a new style in furnituremaking.

Thonet's work became a central, early core around which the great period of modern furniture design could build. It was unique in solving so many pressing problems at one and the same time, uniting beauty of form, inexpensiveness, and versatility. The great pioneers of modern architecture either measured their own work against Thonet chairs—or sat down on them. Poul Henningsen characterized architects' admiration for bentwood furniture very aptly in 1927: "If an architect makes this chair five times more expensive, half as comfortable, and a quarter so beautiful, he can make a name for himself."

97. Le Corbusier. Living room in the Pavillon de l'Esprit Nouveau, Exposition Internationale des Arts Décoratifs, Paris. 1925. The pioneers of modern architecture brought Thonet furniture its greatest acclaim by using it again and again in their exhibitions.

97

98. Café Hawelka on Dorotheergasse, Vienna. Photographed in 1964.
Still popular with artists and students, this café has a fascinating variety of hat stands and cloak racks.

98

The Shakers: Beauty Rests on Utility

As I mentioned in the introduction, those products of the early industrial age that are most important for our time were usually made by anonymous designers. This is particularly true of Shaker furniture, whose forms rested not on considerations of design but on religious principles. Of the many communities founded in America toward the end of the eighteenth century, the Shakers put the idea of the commune into effect the most consequently.

In religious terms the Shaker sect, founded in England in 1747, was perhaps closest to the Quakers and the French Prophets. Their central figure was Mother Ann Lee (1736–84), who joined them in 1774 and emigrated with them to America. In 1787 the community of New Lebanon, New York, was founded, and soon the Shakers began a missionary activity in the course of which many other communities, each organized in ''families,'' were established.

The Shakers consciously left the profane world behind to live in Christian communism and to follow the principles of their faith, which was based on the simultaneous male and female quality of God. Their Kingdom of the Lord on Earth meant to them purity of soul, common ownership, equality of the sexes, and celibacy. They also believed the community should be self-supporting in every way.

The conviction that every unnecessary frill or decoration on an object was sinful and that high quality of craftsmanship contributed to a better life on this earth led the Shakers to reject the capitalist methods of production that dominated the nineteenth century. In contrast to the reform attempts of men like Ruskin and Morris, however, their work was not inimical to technical improvement.

The rules and regulations by which the Shakers lived reveal how important religious and moral beliefs can be, even in terms of furniture design. Among their credos were ''Beauty rests on utility,'' ''Anything may be called perfect which perfectly answers the purpose for which it was designed,'' and ''Every force evolves a form.'' It is particularly this last that evokes, a hundred years before Sullivan's much-quoted ''Form follows function,'' the modern principle of functionalism.

By 1825 nineteen independent Shaker communities had been established; by 1850 they numbered about 6000 people. Their economic organization, based on faith and

99. Shaker dance in the Meeting House, New Lebanon, New York. Mid-nineteenth century.

Not long after the sect was founded in Manchester, England, the lively dances that were a part of their religious ceremonies had earned them the nickname of ''Shaking Quakers.'' ''Their religious service did not consist of prayer and preaching but took the form of a meeting of the faithful, in which the brothers and sisters danced and sang, separately or in groups, but without the men and women touching each other. Among the Shakers the ecstatic dances were gradually replaced by more austere forms, processions and 'marches' in choreographically ordered groups, which, however, still allowed satisfaction of the individual's desire for free personal self-expression'' (Wend Fischer).[7]

100. Price list of Shaker chairs. c. 1880.
Large-scale production of chairs, armchairs, and rockers based on simple, traditional models had first to fill the needs of the rapidly growing Shaker community. Manufacture in series started in New Lebanon in 1852; later, chair parts were farmed out to workshops outside the community, the Shakers only assembling the finished product. Not until 1935 did the last of the chairmakers in Mount Lebanon—Sarah Collins—cease production.

99

100

101

101. Shaker dining hall, Watervliet, New York. c. 1880.
Rules passed down orally from generation to generation, but also law codes (such as the *Millennial Laws,* 1823), governed building style, furnishings, the number of pieces of furniture to be used in bedrooms, size of mirrors, and also colors (e.g., of curtains). "Odd or fanciful styles of architecture, may not be used among Believers, neither should any deviate widely from the common styles of building among Believers, without the union of the Ministry'' (*Millennial Laws,* Section IX, 2).

102. Catalogue page with Shaker chairs. Robert M. Wagan published the first sales catalogue for chairs in 1874. It was he, too, who built a new, large factory in Mount Lebanon in 1873 (its name had been changed from New Lebanon in 1861), equipped it with steam-driven machines, organized sales, and above all standardized and numbered the products. The catalogue appeared almost unchanged for about forty years.

102

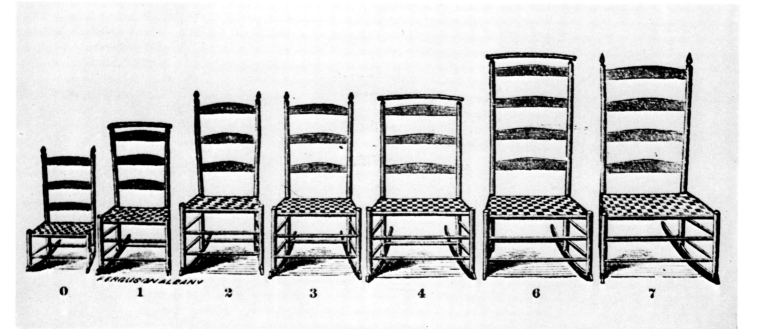

103

104

103. Micajah Burnett. Shaker Meeting House, Pleasant Hill, Kentucky. 1820.
Since purity and simplicity were among the highest virtues for the Shakers, their dwellings were built according to strict rules and left undecorated: "No buildings may be painted white, save meeting houses" (*Millennial Laws,* Section IX,6). Shaker craftsmen, in performing the same tasks over and over again, became extremely skilled, as the technical perfection of their buildings and interiors shows.

104. Shaker "Rules for Visitors." Original in the Shaker Museum, Auburn, Kentucky.

106. Shaker furniture and household objects. American Museum in Britain, Bath, England.
Together with chairs the wooden boxes (on the chest of drawers), containing medicinal herbs and packets of seeds, were among the Shakers' most desired products. These oval boxes made of maplewood cut into strips, usually with bottoms and tops of pine, were made in different sizes and sold in sets called "nests." As in other areas, the Shakers invented simple machines to aid production very early (about 1830).

The clean design of their furniture did justice to the Shakers' beliefs and rules, just as its function filled the needs of the community. Their simple forms were achieved only after years of searching for ever more functional solutions. Teams were formed to do certain tasks, trading off their work from time to time with other teams.

105

105. Shaker dress, New Lebanon, New York. c. 1875. Raw shot silk in gray, lined with brown cotton material. The Shaker Museum, Old Chatham, New York.
Bed, Pleasant Hill, Kentucky. Last half of the nineteenth century. Polished maple. Shakertown at Pleasant Hill, Kentucky.
Chair. c. 1860. Pine, stained reddish-brown, with woven seat of black and green material. The Shaker Museum, Sabbathday Lake, Maine.

106

107. Shaker rocking chair, New Lebanon, New York. c. 1850. Maple with blue-and-white striped cloth seat. Shaker Community, Inc., Hancock, Massachusetts.

108. Shaker folding table, Shirley, Massachusetts. c. 1840–50. Cherry. Fruitlands Museum, Harvard, Massachusetts.

109. Shaker rocking chair. After 1876. Bentwood with olive-colored cloth seat. Elmer R. Pearson Collection, Chicago.
The Shakers probably saw Thonet bentwood chairs at the 1876 Centennial Exhibition in Philadelphia, where they showed their products, and were inspired to experiment along similar lines.

combined with a Puritan way of life, determined the simple forms of their buildings and modest interiors; it was also responsible for their inventive spirit, their early use of industrial methods, and the simplicity of their tools. Of the many objects which the Shakers manufactured and sold in order to purchase what they needed from outside, their furniture was perhaps the most notable in terms of quality and inexpensiveness. On the basis of the simple furniture and tools of colonial America, the Shakers developed a standard line of furniture which, though artless in formal terms, was produced by a division of labor in an early industrial sense that grew out of the principles of the community. Their interiors, such as those that may be seen today in museums at Hancock, Massachusetts; Pleasant Hill, Kentucky; or Bath in England (Plates 111, 113, 106) are, with respect to their simplicity, logic, and functional rightness (this also in a moral sense), as unusual as they are exemplary for the nineteenth century. Here, spiritual values pointed the way to a unity of form and construction, and acceptance of the machine was a matter of course. Only after the Civil War, when the Shaker sect began to decline, did stylistic influences from the outside world begin to make themselves felt.

110

111

110. Shaker table to hold screws and nails, and work chair with revolving seat. Shaker Community, Inc., Hancock, Massachusetts. "Applied to concrete things, to the material environment, it meant that every single object should be so designed as to fulfill its purpose simply and perfectly, and fit harmoniously as an integral part into the order of the surrounding objects. The sense and purpose of each object lies in its utility. An object is therefore perfect when it is perfectly adapted to its intended use. Not 'form' but utility was the Shaker's aim: form was regarded as the result of a design that has achieved the aim of perfect utility in an object" (Wend Fischer).[8]

111. Shaker chest of drawers with hinged top, probably from a sewingroom. Shaker Community, Inc., Hancock, Massachusetts.

◁ 112. Built-in Shaker closet in the Meeting House, Hancock, Massachusetts. c. 1830. Shaker Community, Inc., Hancock, Massachusetts.
Wherever possible, the Shakers used built-in closets, usually of pine.

113

113. Shaker room with bookcase (with hinged writing desk), stove, chairs, and Shaker boards. Shakertown at Pleasant Hill, Kentucky.

The pegboards known as Shaker boards —with tapered wooden hooks or pegs with disc-shaped knobs—were for hanging up clothes and various other objects (in one building in Pleasant Hill more than 6000 pegs were counted). Even chairs and other light furniture were hung on these pegs, while the floors were cleaned. Although the first Shaker buildings had the open fireplaces common in America, later they began to make simple iron stoves, cast in three parts, which they placed in the center of the room. Their long stovepipes gave off a great deal of warmth and helped to save fuel.

The Theories of William Morris and the Challenge of Industry

114

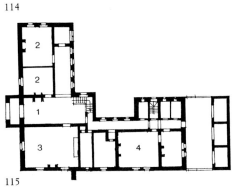

115

During the first half of the nineteenth century organic styles like Empire and Biedermeier still remained relatively pure, despite the fact that furniture manufacturers had begun turning more and more to the past. Historicism soon became the dominant "style" of the nineteenth century, and was accepted by the bourgeoisie and the aristocracy alike. Depending on current fashion or theoreticians' demands, furniture companies borrowed from the world of Gothic, Renaissance, Baroque, or Rococo. Their methods, however, had undergone a considerable change since those bygone ages of fine craftsmanship; though the best pieces continued to be made by hand, machines were used to turn out cheap imitations of them by the thousands. Ironically, the men who pioneered industrial production created, using new methods and new materials, furniture in outmoded forms.

The historians and architects of the day, to judge by their voluminous writings, had a difficult time understanding this deep chasm that had opened up between modern production methods and traditional aesthetics. While as late as Chippendale's day furnituremaking was still considered a craft (in the Middle Ages *every* artist had been a craftsman), now, with more and more useful objects being machine-made and the artist-craftsman dying out, a new concept was needed to describe the activity of giving form to industrial products. The term coined was "industrial design," and among the first to use it was Henry Cole (1808–82). As adviser to Prince Albert, Cole was largely responsible for the Great Exhibition of 1851 and the building of Paxton's Crystal Palace. He devoted his life to improving the quality of machine products, which, despite the fact that they were made in modern factories, were meant to look as if they were handmade. Cole pointed out some of the ways of going about this as early as 1847, in exhibitions sponsored by the Society of Arts and in the *Journal of Design,* which he began to edit in 1849. In reaction to the jarring opposition between the brilliant spatial conception and engineering of the Crystal Palace and the formal chaos of the goods exhibited there, Cole helped found a museum for factory products in 1857, located in South Kensington. Christened the Museum of Applied Art, it was later to be the seed of the Victoria and Albert Museum. Its collection of the best arts and crafts of all ages and nations, it was hoped, would inspire English designers to new ideas and new ways to put them into practice.

The importance of Henry Cole and his comrades-in-arms, among whom was Owen Jones, the painter, lay in their positive attitude to industry. For them, unlike William Morris, the depressing quality of machine-made goods was no reason to condemn the machine, but to improve products precisely in order to make full use of the machine's untried possibilities. Consequently, they advocated better training for designers, but the program suggested remained, unfortunately, only a halfway measure, since they continued to borrow ornament from past styles. Jones did attempt in his main work, however (*The Grammar of Ornament,* published in London in 1856), to set down the laws governing the structure of natural objects such as trees, flowers, and leaves.

114. Philip Webb. Red House, Upton, Bexley Heath, Kent, 1859.
The residence of William Morris from 1860 to 1865. It was built to test his idea that a building could be a work of art, with its architecture subservient to all the other arts it contained. Despite its relation to the irregular-plan dwellings and cloister buildings of the Middle Ages (though with sash windows of the eighteenth century), it turned out to be a quite individual if modest-looking home.

115. Red House, floor plan. 1: entry hall, 2: living rooms, 3: dining room, 4: kitchen·

116. Red House, stairway and hall.

116

In the second half of the nineteenth century a great step forward was taken under the banner of John Ruskin (1819–1900) and William Morris (1834–96). Ruskin, a prolific writer and art historian, dealt not only with architecture and art but with social and economic problems, giving an astounding overview of the entire artistic and social context of his age. He saw the Industrial Revolution in negative terms, holding it responsible for the slow disintegration of what he felt was an organic social order. In his search for harmony he came to believe that art and society (or craftsmanship and society) had been ideally integrated during the Early Middle Ages and thus recommended their example to his contemporaries. Despite his criticism of the industrial products of his day there are passages in his compendious writings that uncannily predict later developments in architecture (and, by analogy, furnituremaking): "Theoretically there is no reason why iron could not be used just as well as wood, and probably the time is not far when a system of new architectural laws will be set out that is entirely dependent on metal construction."[9]

William Morris started where Ruskin left off, in that he attempted to put some of his ideas into practice. He was a socialist, and the results of machine production were thus for him not only tasteless, but a logical consequence of the capitalist system. He set out to fight it on both social and aesthetic grounds; one of his central demands, for instance, was that the huge and overcrowded industrial towns be replaced by smaller communities where fine craftsmanship could again flourish. This idea, incidentally, is very similar to that of men like Robert Owen, who at the same time as Morris were attempting to repair the worst evils of the precapitalist epoch by what they called "industrial villages." It was an idea that led by a direct path to the Garden City movement in England, which represented the first serious attempt to improve living conditions for the working classes.

Being an eminently practical man, one of the first things Morris did was build his own house (Plates 114–117). Begun in 1859 with the help of the architect Philip Webb, his Red House had a floor plan that was out of the ordinary simply by not

117

117. Red House, entry hall.
The furniture, designed by Morris and his friends, was heavy and borrowed strongly from medieval forms. Perfection of craftsmanship was Morris's first commandment. The scene on the large wall cabinet was painted by Edward Burne-Jones.
"Cole and his friends believed in industrial art for the masses, Morris in craftsmanship—and although Morris thought of 'the people' in his creations they remained accessible only to few, for craftsmanship is always costly. Nonetheless, Morris recognized what Cole, Redgrave, Semper, and Wyatt did not see: that designing is not only an aesthetic problem but also an integral part of a larger social problem, and this thought became prophetic" (Nikolaus Pevsner).[10]

118

118. Morris & Co. The Green Dining Room. 1867. Stained-glass window by Edward Burne-Jones. Victoria and Albert Museum, London.

The design of this room was largely in Philip Webb's hands. It is an excellent example of the cooperation between artist and craftsman that Morris was after. "Mr. Morris as managing partner laid down the law, and all his clients had to take it or leave it. The creations were first-class, the artistic and craftsmanly quality outstanding, the prices high. There was no concession to other or even lesser taste. Price reductions were out of the question" (Barbara Morris).[11]

119. Morris & Co. Chair. c. 1866. Ebony-stained oak. Victoria and Albert Museum, London.
A comfortable chair on casters; the backrest is adjustable.

120. Morris & Co. Chair. c. 1865. Ebony-stained birch with woven seat. Victoria and Albert Museum, London.
This chair, manufactured for over eighty years, was based on a form found in Sussex. In 1914 it cost less than 10 shillings.

121. Arthur Heygate Mackmurdo. Writing stand. c. 1886. Oak. The William Morris Gallery, Walthamstow, London.
Mackmurdo, a student of Ruskin's, had a very strong influence with his progressive ideas about architecture, design, and the graphic arts between 1880 and 1890. He was instrumental in the development of Art Nouveau.
This writing stand, designed about 1886 and stylistically a result of Mackmurdo's study of Japanese art, is a radically new solution in terms of construction and truth to materials.

having been conceived to fit one of the stereotyped neo-Renaissance facades that were then in fashion, but developed out of the functional relations between the rooms. When it came to furnishings, Morris realized with all the force of an optical demonstration how shoddy the available furniture was—factory-made chairs were formally and qualitatively inferior; handmade ones were overloaded with historical decor. So Morris and his friends sat down and designed all their own furnishings themselves, a seemingly simple enough idea, but one that paved the way for all the Werkstätten and Craft Guilds to come.

Out of the shared work on this project grew a circle of artists and architects who now devoted themselves to learning the crafts. In 1861 Morris & Company was established to produce household goods of all kinds and of the highest standard (Plates 118–120). Morris's insistence on quality, his advocacy of social justice, and his dynamic personality gave him an influence over the architectural history of the next fifty years that was no less strong for his condemnation of the machine, which he saw as destructive of both art and society, or the backward-looking ideology and idealization of medieval crafts to which it led. Morris's theory and practice were actually mutually contradictory. It was easy enough to say, "I do not want art for the few, as little as education for the few or freedom for the few";[12] but putting it into

119

120

121

effect was entirely another thing. Simply demanding the unity of craftsmanship and art was not enough.

The products of Morris's workshop were luxuries simply because his standards were too high. Quality goods for the masses on this level remained a desirable but unattainable goal. Morris's immediate followers probably could not understand the prophecy contained in the following words of his, written as they surely must have been under the influence of dealings with his clients: "I am not saying that we should endeavor to eliminate all machines; I should like only that many things that are today made by hand be made by machine, and others that are today fabricated by machine be made by hand. In short, we must be masters of our machines and not their slaves, as we are now. We must not liberate ourselves from some material machine or other of steel or brass, but from that huge, immaterial machine of commercial tyranny that oppresses all of our lives."[13]

The workshops Morris founded were the first in a long line of similar experiments in combining art and craft in accordance with the medieval ideal of a community of craftsmen. In the twenty years that followed a number of enterprises devoted to this renaissance were called into life. In 1882, for example, Arthur Hcygate Mackmurdo (1851–1942, Plate 121) established his Century Guild, a studio for interior furnishings, "no longer to entrust all branches of art to the merchant but to the artist." It pursued goals very much like those of Morris & Company, and many of the forms they created in furniture led later, under Mackmurdo's influence, to Art Nouveau.

A number of these societies, among them Morris's (which had been reorganized in 1875), the Century Guild, and the Guild and School of Handicraft of Charles Robert Ashbee (1863–1942, Plate 122), came together in 1888 in the Arts and Crafts Exhibition Society, founded to provide a forum for discussion. Almost all the main representatives of the English avant-garde of the time belonged to it and participated in the exhibitions it soon began sponsoring (Plate 123). Underlying all its efforts was still Morris's ideal of community. As time went on, the Arts and Crafts Exhibition Society's interest began to concentrate more and more on the just and fitting use of materials, and on simplicity and functionality in design—and less and less on the creation of new forms by gifted individuals. Thus, it formed a counterbalance to the Art Nouveau of the Continent, which had reached the flamboyant stage, and prefigured many of the tendencies of the later Sachlichkeit—tendencies that in the rest of Europe had to wait until Art Nouveau had waned. Little by little the negative attitude to machine production began to change, too, and the ideas of Morris and his immediate follower, Walter Crane (1845–1915), had given way by the end of the century to the brute fact that the machine was here to stay. Furniture companies had begun to employ good designers in greater numbers by this time, and since population growth was extremely rapid and becoming more so, they probably realized that there was no alternative to mass production. The idea of cooperating with industry slowly gained acceptance, at least in theory, and designers began to see their task as improving standard products and lending them, as far as it was possible, artistic quality (Plate 124).

124. Liberty & Co., London. Bedroom. 1897.
The influence of the Arts and Crafts movement on furniture design was not very widespread. In addition to the Heal and Son furniture factory managed by Ambrose Heal, who for decades was able to turn many of the movement's ideas to commercial success, it was mainly the Liberty & Co. department store—founded in 1875 by Arthur Lasenby Liberty—that contributed to its popularization. Known initially for the sale of objects, mostly fashionable, from the Orient and the Far East, it later played a central role in spreading Art Nouveau to the Continent (in Italy it became known as *Stile Liberty*).

122. Charles Robert Ashbee. Cabinet. 1889. Oak, painted and gilded. Made by the Guild of Handicraft, Abbotsholme School, Rochester, England.
The early pieces made by the Guild of Handicraft were characterized by simple forms. True to Morris's teachings, Ashbee tried to support his craft activities by farming, and moved the Guild in 1902 out into the country to Chipping Campden, Gloucestershire. His intention, however, to reform industrial society with the aid of arts and crafts was doomed to failure.

123. Arts and Crafts Exhibition, 1890. From left to right: furniture by Ford Madox Brown, R. Blomfield, Ernest Gimson, and W.R. Lethaby.
The slogan "arts and crafts" that was later to become so important was popularized by this group's exhibitions. Like Morris's, their main goals were reform of society and cooperative work. Their expensive and already outmoded production methods, however, led industry to turn out only cheap imitations of their pieces.

124

125. William Burges. Sideboard. Painted decoration by E.J. Poynton. Exhibited in 1862 at the International Exhibition. Victoria and Albert Museum, London.
This piece particularly impressed viewers of the time by its simplicity of construction. Burges, a friend of Godwin's, who advocated an "early English" style of furnishing, was also one of the first collectors of Japanese prints.

In the wake of Morris and his movement, a new variety of Historicism arose in England during the seventies and eighties of the last century—Art Furniture. Charles Lock Eastlake, the movement's most important defender, warned against all formal exaggeration and demanded simple lines and straightforward construction in furniture. He recommended, for example, that the natural grain of untreated wood be retained wherever possible. Nikolaus Pevsner writes, "The expression 'Art Furniture' is significant. It shows that in the second third of the nineteenth century a break had occurred between craftsmanship and art, between artwork and industrial manufacture."[14]

The "Anglo-Japanese" furniture by Edward William Godwin (1833–86) illustrated in the William Watt Factory catalogue of 1877 stood in sharp contrast to the Gothic-derived designs of William Burges (1827–81), whose elaborate and costly pieces really must be reckoned to Art Furniture and thus to Historicism (Plate 125).

Charles Francis Annesley Voysey (1857–1941) was close in design terms to the Arts and Crafts Exhibition Society, having taken over the formal language of his teacher, Arthur Mackmurdo, and developed out of it his own geometric and purist style. In the residences he designed in the tradition of English country houses, Voysey did without the slightest ornamental frill. His rooms derived their effect solely from their necessary elements; they were decidedly functional but interestingly proportioned: "Simplicity requires perfection in all parts; everything artificial

126

127

126. Charles F.A. Voysey. Living room of the architect's house, The Orchard, Chorleywood. 1899.

127. Exterior of the architect's house, The Orchard, Chorleywood. 1899.
Voysey's country houses—he designed very few other types of building—are always related to the surrounding landscape. They are modest buildings with floor plans in which the rooms are lined up one next to the other in a simple way. His thoughts invariably point out the relation between man and architecture. He says, "Peace, joy, simplicity, breadth, warmth, a serene port in the storm, domestic happiness, an economical character, fitting into the environment, a lack of dark passages or corners, an even temperature, and that the house be a suitable frame for its occupants."[15]

is easy by comparison." The first furniture from Voysey's hand, in 1893, was suffused with the same principle and found a strong echo all over Europe. About 1900, in the heyday of Art Nouveau, Voysey was considered on the Continent to be the leading English furniture designer (Plates 128, 129). His houses, built functionally from inside to outside, became known in Germany through Hermann Muthesius as the type of the modern English country house (Plates 126, 127, 130).

Another strong outside influence on the theories of design being discussed in late-nineteenth-century Europe was the art and architecture of Japan, which had been widely publicized by this time. From the vantage point of Europe, it seemed to many people that Japan had somehow managed to retain that medieval harmony of art and society so desired by the troubled West. Few realized that the points of departure were quite different, if not diametrically opposed: in Europe, the will to progress set free by two revolutions; in Japan, a conservative tradition in culture that had grown slowly throughout a long period of social and political stagnation.

The Japanese house, to take only one example, was the product of many cultural influences. Philosophy and religion, the impermeability of social classes, the politics of an economically declining shogun rule, the climate, and ancient tradition all had contributed to its configuration. During the centuries-long Tokugawa regime (1603–1867) it had been subjected to strict norms; certain types of house were reserved for certain estates, and the building laws were very stringent—that extended even to many of its individual parts. Though in Japanese philosophy only a "temporary shelter," the house became not only a work of art in itself but a stage for a highly artificial form of life. Everything in it had its place and its deep significance. The unity of interior space and nature, of space and man, of nature and man was perfect. Japanese rooms, their size determined by the standard *tatami* mats (91 x 182 cms.), could be enlarged at will or opened up to the garden outside by means of sliding doors. Most had no set purpose but were interchangeable. Living in a Japanese house did not require much furniture; room and furniture were one (Plate 134).

The first products of Japanese culture to reach the West (aside from porcelain), the woodcuts which so fascinated the French Impressionists, bore eloquent witness to this brilliant reduction of means. How much greater a sensation the simplicity and

129. Charles F.A. Voysey. Armchair. c. ▷ 1897. Collection Mrs. J. Bottard.
The traditions of the Arts and Crafts movement are particularly evident in Voysey's furniture. Simple, functional forms predominate; the details are carefully articulated. "Poor people's furniture for the rich," they were once derisively called, but grace and perfection of form are characteristic of their creator.

130. Charles F.A. Voysey. Stairway in the ▷ Horniman House, Chelsea, London. 1906.

perfection of the Japanese house must have been to people used to murky interiors overloaded with pseudo-historical furniture! James Abbott McNeill Whistler (1834–1903) and Edward William Godwin (1833–86, Plates 131–133, 135, 136), with the literary support of Oscar Wilde, were among the first artists to attempt a translation of Japanese conceptions of form and space into Western terms. With Voysey, and even more strongly with Mackintosh, abstraction became the content of new and individual approaches to the design of interior space.

The influence of the Japanese house remained strong throughout the development of modern architecture. We know, for instance, that long before he built the Imperial Hotel in Tokyo, Frank Lloyd Wright had visited Japan several times; the open plan and projecting roof of his Prairie Houses point more to Japan than to his immediate predecessors in America, such as Richardson. Later, Richard Neutra transplanted the Far Eastern unity of interior and exterior space to the supercivilization of California. The continuing challenge of Japanese architecture and its influence on modern architectural thought is a theme that runs through the writings of Walter Gropius, as it does through the early years of the Bauhaus and the Far Eastern mysticism that played such a great role there.

128. Charles F.A. Voysey. Writing desk with hinge bands of copper. 1896. Victoria and Albert Museum, London.
"Let us start by getting rid of the profusion of useless ornament and burning the modish finery which disfigures our furniture and our household utensils. Let us cut down the number of patterns and colors in one room. Let us give up all imitations, and allow each element of the furnishing to be the best of its kind" (Voysey, 1893).[16]

130

129

132

131

131. Edward William Godwin. Cabinet. c. 1876. Walnut with inlaid carvings of Japanese boxwood. Victoria and Albert Museum, London.

132. Edward William Godwin. White House, for James McNeill Whistler, Chelsea, London. 1877.
Godwin's own house was described by a contemporary in the following words: "He had painted the walls of his rooms in simple colors, hung up a few scattered Japanese woodcuts, and laid a few Turkey carpets on the bare floor."[17]
These first attempts to apply Japanese formal thought and construction principles to European interior design, though they indeed had something bizarre about them, were extremely important in clearing rooms of Victorian clutter.

133. Edward William Godwin. Chair. c. 1885. Oak painted black. Made by William Watt. Victoria and Albert Museum, London. Coffee table. 1874. Oak painted black. Made by William Watt. City Art Gallery, Bristol.

134

133

135, 136. Edward William Godwin. Furniture designs for the Art Furniture Warehouse, London. 1877.

Japonisme was spread during the last half of the nineteenth century in England not only by the painter James McNeill Whistler and the writer Oscar Wilde, but also later by the drawings of Aubrey Beardsley (1872–98). In architecture and interior design some of the first attempts in this direction, such as the White House that Godwin built for Whistler in 1877—a simple, white cube —were of great importance. The Japanese aspect of this design is expressed only indirectly, in the clarity of its outline.

◁134. *Ura senke* tea-ceremony school, Kyoto, Japan.

The simple, clear conception of Japanese rooms and the craftsmanlike use of materials in their natural form have influenced the formal thinking of many Western architects up to the present day.

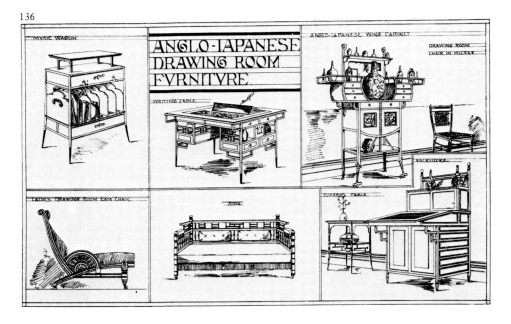

136

Art Nouveau—Overcoming Historicism

While in England the Arts and Crafts movement and its followers had given furniture simple, strong forms without, however, completely divesting it of historical influences, on the Continent toward the end of the nineteenth century the first attempts were being made to create a new world of form independent of all traditional styles. Early forms of Art Nouveau, as the movement came to be known, had already appeared in English printing and book illustration about mid-century, and English ideas—those of Ruskin and Morris—again provided the inspiration for a return to natural forms in decoration as an antidote to the ugliness of the industrialized world (Plates 137, 138). The goal of both theory and practice was no less than to transform man's entire environment by applied art.

Art Nouveau had its first successes in Belgium. Its representatives there—foremost Gustave Serrurier-Bovy (1858–1910, Plate 139), Victor Horta (1861–1947, Plates 140, 141), and Henri van de Velde (1863–1957)—held closely to English models at first, but they soon succeeded in overcoming the linear quality of English Art Nouveau and translating it into three-dimensional terms. Around 1890 Serrurier-Bovy began experimenting with furniture designs which initially were clearly inspired by the austere Arts and Crafts furniture, but soon found their own formal language. Victor Horta, possibly the most important artist of Belgian Art Nouveau, designed a series of houses between 1892 and 1900 that in terms of style, plan, and construction—making full use of iron and glass for residential buildings—were far ahead of their time. He succeeded in bringing together seminal ideas and Art Nouveau motifs to form a rhythmic whole, a *Gesamtkunstwerk* of the

137. Arthur Heygate Mackmurdo. Title page for *Wren's City Churches*. 1883.[18]

138

138. Arthur Heygate Mackmurdo. Chair. Before 1885.[19]
Mackmurdo's planar ornaments and extenuated, flamelike curving lines influenced Continental Art Nouveau. Though ornament of this kind was very common on English printed fabrics or wallpapers about 1880, Mackmurdo's furniture ornaments stood in contrast to the clear forms of Voysey.

139. Gustave Serrurier-Bovy. Exhibition room. Between 1894 and 1898.
The architect and cabinetmaker Serrurier-Bovy offered for sale at his shop in Lüttich furniture and arts and crafts, including wallpapers and fabrics by William Morris, as early as 1890.

Henri van de Velde noted in his memoirs that Serrurier-Bovy "was the first on the Continent to create furniture according to new aesthetic principles."

139

141. Victor Horta. Stairwell, Hôtel Tassel, Brussels. 1892–93.

The stairwell in Horta's first masterpiece, the Hôtel Tassel, points the way to the formal language to come, with its use of free-standing iron supports with "floral capitals" and the linear ornaments on the walls; but its daring spatial composition, determined by glass and iron, presages developments far beyond Art Nouveau.

140

141

140. Victor Horta. Sideboard and cabinet, dining room of the Hôtel Solvay, Brussels. 1895–1900.

Though Horta (as Henri van de Velde notes in his memoirs) bought the furnishings for his Hôtel Tassel from English arts-and-crafts firms, for the Hôtel Solvay he designed everything himself, down to the last detail in accord with his overall conception. The forms and construction of his furniture owe much to the tradition of French furnituremaking (Rococo) and thus to Art Nouveau of French provenance.

highest originality and quality. It is no wonder that Art Nouveau proper is often said to have begun with the building of his first house, Hôtel Tassel, in 1892–93.

Though Henri van de Velde was an architect by trade, his fame lies in his interior and furniture design (Plates 142, 148), his ornaments and type faces, and his theoretical writings. He was more rigorous than any other Art Nouveau artist in rejecting stylistic elements of the past (Horta, by contrast, often quoted from French Rococo), and he turned away from purely floral forms early on. Inspired by Serrurier-Bovy and English models, he found a furniture style based on the contrast between curving lines and smooth, filled planes, to the point of often putting almost too much emphasis on construction. In the furnishings of his own home (built in 1892), the four rooms of the S. Bing gallery in Paris, and particularly the houses he decorated after his return to Germany, he showed himself a master not only of the tense line of the graphic artist but of the sure, subdued hues of the painter (like many architects of the day, van de Velde had started as a painter). He took the theory of Art

Nouveau literally, that change was necessary in *all* areas of life, and hence did not restrict himself to designing houses and interiors but applied his craft to useful objects of all kinds—including clothing—forcing them, if necessary, to fit the formal laws he devised. Van de Velde was out not only to redesign furniture, but the very lives of its users.

Furniture did not play nearly as great a part in French Art Nouveau as it did in Belgian. Émile Gallé (1846–1904, Plates 152, 153), Louis Majorelle (1859–1926, Plate 155), Hector Guimard (1867–1942, Plates 149, 150), Eugène Gaillard (1862–1933, Plate 151), and Eugène Vallin (Plate 154) were not able to break completely with the great tradition of French furnituremaking. With its exaggeration of form, its tectonic construction, and its pictorial adjuncts—inlay work, for example—the furniture of French Art Nouveau did not belie its heritage of the rich Rococo tradition. A high value was placed on the skilled craftsmanship that had been handed down for centuries; the emphasis was not on the integrated design of entire rooms, but on individual pieces and beautiful materials.

In Scotland about 1890, Charles Rennie Mackintosh (1868–1928) and his group,

142. Workshop of the Société van de Velde in Ixelles. c. 1899, (In the right foreground, Henri van de Velde).

Despite all his appreciation for the problems of the Industrial Age, which appeared in a certain acceptance of the machine and particularly in his views on society, Henri van de Velde was not able to escape the conditions of his time. If his furniture designs, by reason of their hyperfunctionalism, were a challenge to old styles and an attempt to create a new one, their expensive methods of manufacture nevertheless limited them to a small circle of the well-to-do. Since the exclusive use of handwork and high demands on quality left almost no room for profit, his studio, like other, similar enterprises—such as the Wiener Werkstätten, often faced financial ruin. "I admitted that I was determined to follow Ruskin and Morris on their path until their prophecy was realized—the return of beauty on earth and the dawn of an era of social justice and human dignity" (Henri van de Velde).[20]

143

143. Henri van de Velde. Dining room in the house of Harry Graf Kessler, Weimar. 1902–3.

144. Henri van de Velde. Sewing table and armchair. c. 1900.

Van de Velde made many versions of this armchair with different upholstery. He did not have the wooden parts "bent" but cut out of boards—a process that stood in contradiction to his functional thinking. And yet the plastic articulation of the forms and the lines of ornament on the fabric give this chair a surprising formal unity. Despite its sculptural quality, the sewing table illustrated has been designed to serve its function well; ease of movement is ensured by the casters, close work is aided by the cutouts in the table top, and accessibility by the swing-out drawers.

144

145

145. Henri van de Velde. Dining-room chair with wicker seat in Haus Bloemenwerf, Uccle, Brussels. 1895.

Even in the first chairs that van de Velde designed for his house in Uccle, his basic principle is apparent: each individual part is functionally overemphasized and, without respect for the demands of the material, fitted into a framework that could be described as a drawing in three dimensions.

146. Henri van de Velde. Desk. c. 1900.

the Four—Mackintosh; his wife, Margaret Macdonald Mackintosh; Margaret's sister Frances Macdonald McNair; and Frances's husband, Herbert McNair—began to create their own aesthetic world. Though this little community devoted itself mainly to interiors and the design of furniture, a number of Mackintosh's buildings, particularly the Glasgow School of Art, made architectural history (Plates 156–160). The slender, geometric forms favored by this group stood in sharp contrast to the almost rustic simplicity of contemporaneous English furniture, though their light-filled, usually ivory-colored interiors had much in common with those of Voysey. Strong Japanese influence was paired with original stylistic touches that are difficult to compare with anything that had gone before. Perhaps most characteristic of the Glasgow School were forms based on straight lines and rectangles combined with a gently curving, linear ornament, applied both to furniture and interior walls—a style without parallel in Continental Art Nouveau.

Mackintosh participated in 1900 in an exhibition of the Vienna Secession, which had been founded just three years previously and in which Joseph Maria Olbrich (1867–1908, Plates 161, 162) and Josef Hoffmann (1870–1956, Plates 163, 164)

146

147

148

147. Henri van de Velde. Gentleman's study, Haus Hohenhof, Hagen, Westphalia. 1906.

"The character of all my commercial and ornamental designs springs from a single source: reason and reasonableness in being and appearance. . . . What has to be done is find a new basis from which we can create a new style; the seed of this style, which I see clearly in my mind's eye, is this: to create nothing that does not have a reasonable *raison d'être*" (Henri van de Velde).[21]

148. Henri van de Velde. Lady's sitting room, Haus Hohenhof, Hagen, Westphalia. 1906.

149. Hector Guimard. Bedroom. c. 1900. Musée des Arts Décoratifs, Paris.

played a central role. It was Mackintosh who stimulated Austrian designers to develop the geometric style that became so typical of them, and which, of all varieties of Art Nouveau, perhaps comes closest to our ideas of design today. The Vienna Werkstätten were founded in 1903; in the thirty years of their existence they made profound contributions to furniture design, and not only in Austria.

In regard to the German variety of Art Nouveau, Jugendstil, the name of Henri van de Velde crops up again, for his influence was very strong on the movement

150. Hector Guimard. Desk, designed for his own house. c. 1903. The Museum of Modern Art, New York, bequest of Mme Hector Guimard.
Guimard, the designer of the Paris Métro stations, called himself ''l'architecte d'art.'' His furniture and architectural designs show connections with Belgian Art Nouveau. Their lines and bands are either purely graphic surface ornament, or they border the volumes of his furniture in a completely unconstructive manner. The extent to which construction, function, and materials were considered secondary may be seen from the fact that many of his pieces were first modeled in plaster.

150

151

151. Eugène Gaillard. Cabinet. 1910. Musée des Arts Décoratifs, Paris.

152. Émile Gallé. Bedroom. c. 1900. Musée de l'École de Nancy.
Émile Gallé, Louis Majorelle, and Eugène Vallin all worked in Nancy. Fine intarsia work in the manner of the French *dix-huitième* characterizes the furniture of this school. In contrast to the clean lines of English Arts and Crafts furniture, the basic forms of their pieces are covered with an abundance of Art Nouveau curlicues.

153. Émile Gallé. Lady's writing desk. Before 1900. Walnut with inlays of various woods. Musée de l'École de Nancy.

154. Eugène Vallin. Dining room. 1903–6. ▷ Musée de l'École de Nancy.

153

152

154

155. Louis Majorelle. Small table. c. 1900. Musée des Arts Décoratifs, Paris.

155

there, following an exhibition in 1897 at Dresden of his interiors for the S. Bing gallery. He moved to Germany in 1899. Among the many commissions he executed there during the following years was the famous Folkwang Museum in Hagen. Another seminal exhibition, which led to the mutual enrichment of German and Austrian Art Nouveau, was that held in Mathildenhöhe in Darmstadt in 1901 under the direction of Olbrich. In Munich, a group formed around Bernhard Pankok (1872–1943, Plates 165, 167), August Endell (1871–1925, plate 166), Bruno Paul (1874–1968, Plate 168), Hermann Obrist (1863–1927, Plate 170), Richard Riemerschmid (1868–1957, Plate 169), and others. At first they worked with strongly floral forms, but slowly found their way to an organic-abstract style. In 1898, the Vereinigte Werkstätten für Kunst und Handwerk were established, which combined in 1907 with the Dresdener Werkstätten to form the Deutsche Werkstätten für Handwerkskunst. The best furniture designer of the group was probably Riemerschmid; following in the footsteps of van de Velde, he graduated from the decorative ornamentation of single pieces to conceiving interiors as a whole, and he also went the furthest of any Art Nouveau furniture designer in the direction of abstraction.

Since most Art Nouveau designers had come from painting, they first had to learn the furnituremaking art. True to Morris's principles, close contacts between artists and craftsmen arose, and designers' demands were high—but, as before, excellent

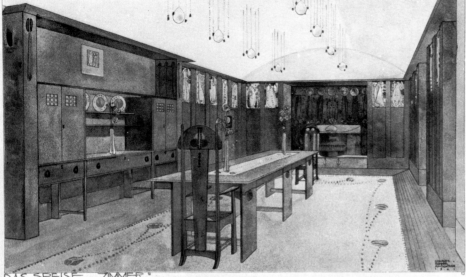

156

158

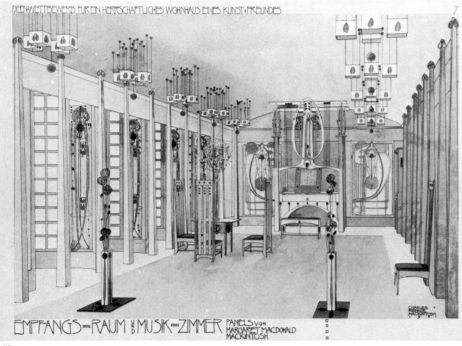

157

159

156, 157. Charles Rennie Mackintosh. Dining room; reception room; and music room in the house of an artlover. Competition design for Alexander Koch Verlag. 1901.

158. Charles Rennie Mackintosh. Reading room in the library of the Glasgow School of Art, as originally furnished with Mackintosh's version of the Windsor chair. 1907–9.

159. Charles Rennie Mackintosh. Chair, probably from the Cranston Tearoom. 1901.

160. Charles Rennie Mackintosh. Entry hall of Hill House, Helensburgh. 1902–3.
Spatial conceptions such as those Mackintosh was able to realize in the library of the Glasgow School of Art, and color schemes such as those he used in the houses he designed—white, with strong pink and lilac tones—went far beyond the limitations of Art Nouveau. The angular construction of his furniture, although certainly chosen for formal reasons, also points the way to the future.
Nevertheless, the attempts to mass-produce Mackintosh's chairs that we are seeing today must be considered as a new flowering of Historicism.

161. Joseph Maria Olbrich. Music room in Das Neue Palais, Darmstadt.

162. Joseph Maria Olbrich. Children's furniture from the princess's house at Schloss Wolfsgarten near Darmstadt. 1902. Collection Prince Ludwig von Hessen.

161

162

craftsmanship was no assurance of the wide appeal they desired. With the exception of the Wiener Werkstätten work of about 1905, which came very close to meeting the requirements of machine production, most Art Nouveau furniture designs were formal successes but technical flops. They could never be truly rational in the sense of using time and materials to best advantage—curved chair legs cut from wide planks, convex doors, and rounded corners on desks and chests may have been beautiful, but they were wasteful. By the time furniture factories had begun to exploit the fashion, Art Nouveau had already passed its peak. Mundane manufacture meshed poorly with esoteric forms; exaggeration, on the other hand, could bring only formal chaos. No doubt Art Nouveau had a wide effect on taste through its many exhibitions and the publicity they attracted, and the writings on interior design, furniture, and general social problems of its more important artists, particularly van

163

163. Josef Hoffmann. Corner of a living room, from *Ver Sacrum 1898–1903*.

164. Josef Hoffmann. Bedroom in a converted farmhouse, Bergerhöhe bei Hohenberg, Lower Austria. 1899.
Olbrich, like Josef Hoffmann, was oriented initially toward England and influenced by the formal diversity of Belgian Art Nouveau. While the music room, with its variety of forms and materials, may be traced back to the ensemble style of the English Arts and Crafts movement, Olbrich's children's furniture shows the influence of the English version of *Japonisme*. For the modest interior of the farmhouse illustrated, Hoffmann even chose an English fabric wall covering to highlight the simple pine paneling.

164

de Velde, forced people to take sides and give the issue of modern design serious thought. The immense élan with which they fought for their ideas and sought a new formal language beyond Historicism are also factors which speak much in their favor.

Furniture and interior design were indeed among the greatest achievements of Art Nouveau. Yet there is no overlooking the fact that even its most progressive architects and artists neglected the most pressing task of their era, which was to save the cities and create humane living conditions for the underprivileged. Though there was no lack of well-meaning attempts to design housing and furniture for workingmen and their families, the discrepancy between the desire for high-quality craftsmanship and commercial necessity was simply too great to be bridged. The few years of Art Nouveau activity were too short to enable artists to go beyond the

165

167

165. Bernhard Pankok. Music salon, created for the World Exhibition, Saint Louis, 1904. Furniture of walnut, piano of old oak. Manufactured by Georg Schöttle Werkstätte in Stuttgart.

Most of the artists who, with Henri van de Velde, became known as the Munich Circle worked for the Vereinigte Werkstätten für Kunst und Handwerk. Both the positive and negative aspects of Art Nouveau were apparent in their designs. They gave their ideas enormous popularity by organizing exhibitions; on the other hand, they tended to formal exaggeration in their furniture, which was picked up willingly by industry and exploited, eventually giving Art Nouveau a bad name. The cooperation of artists, craftsmen, and distributors that they practiced, however, was just as important for the later Deutscher Werkbund as for the ideas of the Weimar Bauhaus.

166

166. August Endell. Bookcase. c. 1900. Walnut. Private collection, Wiesbaden.

167. Bernhard Pankok. Sketch. c. 1900.

168. Bruno Paul. Dining room; exhibited in Dresden, 1906.

168

experimental stage to gradual and careful evaluation and development of their ideas. Thus the decisive factor in the demise of Art Nouveau was its isolation from the new social order—the impossibility, in the last analysis, of integrating the craft ideal into a society that had long accepted the machine. In the end, its exalted world of form was little more than an arts-and-crafts puzzle with ornamental pieces, without relation to the social principles that had grown out of William Morris's teachings.

169. Richard Riemerschmid. Armchair, painted red. c. 1900. Die Neue Sammlung, Munich.

170. Hermann Obrist. Chairs and serving table, from a dining-room set. c. 1898. Moss oak. Private collection, Starnberg.

169

170

Beyond Art Nouveau—Antoni Gaudí, Frank Lloyd Wright, Otto Wagner, Adolf Loos

Few of the pioneers of modern architecture were able to resist the pull of Art Nouveau; in the oeuvres of a handful of strong personalities there are, however, interiors and furniture designs that stem from independent thought.

The work of Antoni Gaudí (1852–1926) has its roots in Catalonian Gothic. He saw his task as adapting for the new age the methods of his ancestors and their truth to materials. Though many of his buildings are reminiscent of Art Nouveau as practiced elsewhere on the Continent, his formal language is really his own, since it never divorced itself from the traditions and the landscape of his native Catalonia.

The sheer force of his architecture and interiors has overshadowed Gaudí's furniture designs. Their rich and sculptural shapes, which seem to have grown organically from their materials, like the freely flowing structures of the Palacio Güell or the freely interpenetrating rooms of the Casa Milá (Plate 174), are the result of a happy combination of Gaudí's imagination with the extraordinary gifts of Catalonian craftsmen. Designs such as the benches in Parque Güell are really sculptures, and the rich play of color and form in their mosaics of glazed tile is like a vision of the future. In Gaudí's furniture (Plates 171–173, 175) we see a first, sculptural solution to problems of construction, structure, and materials of the kind that designers face today, with new materials and manufacturing methods—furniture made of plastic, for example.

Frank Lloyd Wright (1869–1959), thanks to his wide and varied architectural oeuvre, which had already reached a high artistic level by 1900, and his extensive

171. Antoni Gaudí. Chair from Casa Calvet. 1898–1903.
Plastic articulation of a chair fitted together out of solid wood pieces. The seat is scooped out like a shell, the back organically formed. The treatment of the legs —which really goes against all the rules of woodworking—reminds one of the wrought-iron work of Gaudí's chaise longue.

171

172. Antoni Gaudí. Bench from the private apartment of the owner of Casa Battló, Barcelona. 1905–7.
This bench, with its two seats that are carved to fit the body, is really of quite simple construction. Only the freeform backrests placed high demands on the craftsman who made them—he had to be a sculptor in wood.

172

173. Antoni Gaudí. Dining room in Casa ▷ Battló, Barcelona. 1905–7.
The structural, organic forms of the facade continue into the interior and determine all the elements of the room: ceiling, columns, windows, furniture. This middle-class apartment is lifted out of the world of Historicism not only by the free interpenetration of the rooms but by the expressive design of every detail.

174. Antoni Gaudí. Casa Milá, Barcelona, ▷ floor plan. 1905–10.
This free plan, influenced by organic growth patterns, is made possible only by the use of a reinforced concrete skeleton.

175. Antoni Gaudí. Chaise longue, Palacio ▷ Güell. 1885–89. Wrought iron, upholstered with calfhide.
Complete freedom from conventional ideas about construction, choice of materials, and formal language; a traditional type of furniture is transformed into a sculpture that placed the highest imaginable demands on the craftsmen who made it—particularly the ironsmith.

173

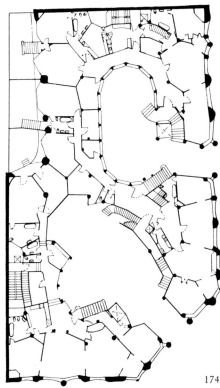

174

175

writings in architectural theory, is today recognized as one of the greatest pioneers of modern architecture. His thoughts on the function of form and material, as well as on the most pressing social problems of his age, are of unique stature (Plates 176–178). Wright's ideas stemmed from very diverse sources. The geometric shapes of the children's games devised by Froebel influenced his visual sense; his childhood impressions of his grandfather's farm left in him a deep love of nature and a feeling for the natural use of materials. His apprenticeship in the office of the greatest American architect of the day, Louis Sullivan, was just as important for his development as his study of Japanese culture. Japan exhibited at the Chicago World Exhibition in 1893 a replica of a typical Japanese building, as a "museum" for paintings and woodcuts (of which Wright himself had an impressive collection). He visited Japan for the first time in 1905. The idea of adapting the open Japanese floor plan to the needs of American suburban architecture, the influence of Richardson's and other still historically dominated, rustic residences, and the English tradition of making the hearth the center of the home—all these factors came together in the 'Prairie Houses Wright designed between 1900 and 1910, his first important contribution to modern architecture.

In his article "Prairie Architecture," published in 1931 in *Modern Architecture,* Wright explained his conception. What was crucial, he wrote, was ". . . to reduce the number of necessary parts of the house and of individual rooms to a minimum and to combine everything into one enclosed space—so arranged that light, air, and vision can permeate the whole with a feeling of unity."[22] All proportions of the house were to be "liberally human." He wanted ". . . to include the furniture as far as possible as organic architecture, to make it one with the building and design it in simple shapes for the machine. Again, straight lines and rectangular forms." In a lecture entitled "The Art and Craft of the Machine," given before the Arts and Crafts Society in Chicago, he emphasized, already in 1901, the importance of simple, clean-lined furniture, giving new meaning to the words of Ruskin and Morris: "The machine makes possible by its wonderful ability to cut, to form, to smooth and to repeat, to work so economically that nowadays the poor as well as the rich can enjoy clear and austere forms in the handling of surface detail that a Sheraton or a Chippendale could only indicate through the costly extravagance of their intarsia work and that the Middle Ages totally ignored. The machine has liberated the beauties of nature in wood and made it possible to put an end to the majority of the senseless martyrdoms to which wood has been subjected since the world began, for, with the exception of the Japanese, it has been misused and mishandled everywhere and by all peoples. Is this not, looked at properly, precisely the process of omission which Morris championed?"[23] This profession of faith in the machine and to materials characterizes Wright's key contribution to furniture design, despite the fact that it may seem too dogmatic to us today.

Otto Wagner (1841–1918) was the true founder of the Vienna School, though its fame may have been due more to such exuberant but really quite contradictory personalities as Adolf Loos, Josef Hoffmann, and Joseph Maria Olbrich. Wagner's oeuvre witnesses his ongoing struggle with the new technical possibilities and social transformations of the turn-of-the-century period—this is as true of his architecture as his furniture. Wagner's first important buildings still stood in the sign of Historicism and, like his own Stadtpalais of 1899, were furnished with Renaissance copies. Following his call to the Vienna Academy in 1894 came a phase of theoretical reorientation. In *Moderne Architektur,* a book he published in 1895, Wagner took the view that modern architecture should grow out of the needs of modern life. He called for a style that should gain its expressive power from its construction and materials. The horizontal line he advocated took visible form in his residences and

176. Frank Lloyd Wright. Armchair. 1904. The Museum of Modern Art, New York. Frank Lloyd Wright attempted to make even his furniture designs "architectural" and "human." He did not always succeed, as his frank self-appraisal shows: "Somehow I always had black and blue spots my whole life long from all too close contact with my own furniture."[24]

177. Frank Lloyd Wright. Living room of the Avery Coonley House, Riverside, Illinois. 1908.

The Prairie Houses of Wright's golden age from 1900 to 1910 were not conceived in terms of individual rooms but as an open interior space focused on a single point, the fireplace. Low ceilings with skylights and the use of similar materials on both facade and interior characterize these houses. The impression of the house as a total work of art is increased by the unity of architectonic form and decoration.

178. Frank Lloyd Wright. Preliminary drawing for the Avery Coonley House, Riverside, Illinois. 1908.

178

office buildings, with the dimensions of the furniture rigorously matched to the height of the wall paneling.

Wagner was a teacher of extraordinary gifts and influence, and his reputation spread far beyond his native Vienna. His most important building, the Post Office Savings Bank in Vienna (1904–6, Plates 96, 179, 180), also houses his great contribution to the furniture art of his era. Though the offices of the management still breathe the air of nineteenth-century Renaissance Revival, the seating he designed for the rest of the building is definitely in the spirit of modern mass production. The chairs in the offices, the armchairs of the auditorium, the stools in the main hall were all executed in the bentwood technique developed in Vienna at the Thonet and Kohn & Kohn factories. It is astonishing that fully fifty years had to pass from the first appearance of mass-produced chairs (Thonet No. 14 in 1859) to their first use by a great modern architect.

The design and technical facilities of the building are on the same high level as the materials used in its interior. In every room Wagner's uncompromising eye for detail and feeling for human proportion are apparent. His Post Office Savings Bank is a characteristic—and positive—example of how good architecture can be in a utilitarian age. The building both functions in a technical sense and works in an aesthetic sense, as even the old and conservative Kaiser Franz Josef was forced to remark at the opening ceremonies: "Odd, how well the people fit in. . . ."

Adolf Loos (1870–1933) was perhaps the prime theoretician of a puritan approach to furniture design and interior space at the turn of the century. The years of 1893 to 1896 he spent in America, during the heyday of the Chicago School, where he

179. Otto Wagner. The Green Room (Vice-Governor's Office), Post Office Savings Bank, Vienna. 1904–6.
The straightforward furnishings of the individual rooms of this building reflect Wagner's constructive bent and blend perfectly with the simple shapes of chairs and tables. The built-in cabinets and clock are integrated into the paneling, which lends the room unity; monotony is avoided by the slightly changing rhythms of the doors.

180. Otto Wagner. Conference room, Post Office Savings Bank, Vienna. 1904–6. Portrait of Kaiser Franz Josef by Wilhelm List (the portraits of the Governors of the Post Office, above the paneling, right, were added later).

Wall paneling and bentwood chairs—made according to Wagner's designs by the then-largest manufacturers of bentwood furniture in Vienna, Gebrüder Thonet and Kohn & Kohn, are stained black, and the fittings of the wall cabinets, armrests, and chair legs are aluminum. The lighting fixtures were altered later; originally, all of the management offices had bare light bulbs arranged in equally spaced sockets.

absorbed the thought of Sullivan and his insight into the relation between form and function. On returning to Vienna he very soon began to direct a vehement attack on all ornament in architecture, particularly of the Art Nouveau variety, citing Sullivan and Wagner in his defense. What Loos wanted to prove was that Art Nouveau ornament was unworthy of the modern age, that a building devoid of ornament symbolized clear thinking, and that forms were beautiful when they expressed their intended function and when all of their elements fused into an indivisible whole—in other words, that decoration was anathema to architecture. In 1908, he wrote in *Ornament und Verbrechen:* "Ornament is squandered work and hence squandered health. And it has always been so. Today, however, it also means squandered material, and both mean squandered capital."[25] Loos's acerbic and frank essays have become central to every theory of modern architecture that has been put forth since they were written. In his earliest writings, which appeared during the Vienna Jubilee Exhibition of 1898, he discussed the whole gamut of daily life in *fin de siècle* Vienna, from men's clothing to interior decoration. Soon the Vienna School of Arts and Crafts and its professors, and later the German Werkbund, had become the target of his attacks. Though many of his polemics can be fully understood only against the background of the Vienna of his day, still Loos's writings are a remarkable achievement, just as relevant today as then. Young furniture designers could do worse than take many of his statements on furniture and interiors to heart.

Adolf Loos furnished about fifty apartments in all, but built only a very few residential buildings and houses. His interiors (Plates 181–184), with their craftsmanlike use of choice materials such as fine woods and marble, were very sparsely furnished. They are not without their contradictions, however; often a clearly articulated interior is compromised by an artificially lowered wood-beam ceiling, and Loos remained true to his beloved Chippendale imitations until the death of his cabinetmaker, Veillich (Plate 181). It was Richard Neutra, in his book *Neues Bauen in der Welt* of 1930, who pointed out Loos's penchant for fake timber ceilings in "golden oak" and fireplaces in the style of Henry Hobson Richardson. Above all, it was unpretentious English furniture that Loos revered his whole life long.

Even within the strict limitations of the apartments he furnished, Loos attempted to realize his conception of interior space by adding niches and fireplaces to main rooms. Not until his Rufer House of 1922, however, did he have the opportunity to put his "space plan" into effect—an idea he had introduced with his Loos House in 1910, an office building in Michaelerplatz, and which he later brought to fruition in his Müller House in Prague (1930). The crux of this concept was planning in three dimensions: "For that is the great revolution in architecture—solving a floor plan in space!"[26] Depending on their function and importance, individual rooms were not only to be of different sizes but on different levels, abutted one to the other to produce a cube-shaped building. His "floor plans in volume" played a large part in shaping even the life styles of the people who lived in them, not to mention the form of their furniture and furnishings.

Surely the clarity of Loos's furniture and the love of materials that manifests itself in every piece would not have been possible without the skilled cabinetmakers of Vienna. Despite all their enmities, a love of fine craftsmanship unites Loos with Josef Hoffmann and the Wiener Werkstätten. The simple home furnishings designed there in and about 1905, still very much under the influence of Mackintosh, are in terms of construction and utilization of materials in every respect the equal of the furniture designed by Adolf Loos.

181

182

181. Adolf Loos. Dining nook in the large living room, Haus Steiner, Vienna. 1910.
The living room, which adjoined the garden, served several purposes—being a combination sitting, dining, and music room. The chairs are remarkable imitations in Chippendale style.

182. Adolf Loos. Extendable table and matching chair (signed). 1898. Mahogany and bronze. Private collection, Switzerland.

183. Adolf Loos. "My wife's bedroom," Loos apartment, Vienna. 1903.
The entire room, except for the blue carpeting, is in white—wardrobes and walls were covered with white batiste. The living room with annex of the Loos residence is now on exhibit in the Historisches Museum der Stadt Wien.

184. Adolf Loos. Die Kärntner Bar (American Bar), Vienna. 1907. ▷
Preserved almost unchanged. Photographs of the time show in place of the landscape a portrait of Peter Altenberg by Gustav Lagerspacher.
The room, only 3.5 x 7.5 m. in size, and 3.5 m. high, is made to look much larger by the mirrors placed between the pilaster strips. Dark mahogany, black leather, brass frames around the glass table tops which are lighted from below, and the coffered ceiling of yellowish brown marble all witness to an extraordinarily fine sense of materials.

183

From Arts and Crafts to Werkbund—the Idea of Community

The building of the Red House by William Morris and his friends (1859, Plates 114–117) signaled the beginning of the development that was to determine the history of architecture and furnishings for decades. Artists and craftsmen all over Europe began to form communities to work on common problems and to discuss the effects of industrialization on art, and what could be done about them. A number of these groups, particularly the Arts and Crafts Society in England, attempted to design furniture and household goods suited to the new era. Its influence on style was enormous, and the idea of community, which it was the first to practice, soon spread across the Continent. The achievements of the numerous societies of artists and artisans that now formed were just as important a step on the path to modern architecture as the personal contributions of its great pioneers.

In Germany and Austria the first of these societies came in with Jugendstil. In 1903 Josef Hoffmann (1870–1956) founded the Wiener Werkstätten, together with Koloman Moser (1868–1916, Plate 186) and Josef Wärndorfer as financier. Hoffmann, who had been a student of Otto Wagner, carried on Wagner's rationalistic approach to architecture without, however, going as far as Adolf Loos to reject all ornament. His main interest was in fine craftsmanship, a subject he taught at the Vienna School of Arts and Crafts. The first years of the Wiener Werkstätten were characterized by a stringent, rectilinear style, with many elements borrowed from Mackintosh and a system of ornament based on the square (which brought its founder the nickname "Square Hoffmann").

The Wiener Werkstätten were no exception in expounding the theories of Morris and Ruskin; nor were they any exception in having largely upper-class clients. Hoffmann's masterpiece, the Palais Stoclet in Brussels of 1911 (Plates 187, 188), was tailored just as much to the needs of *fin de siècle* high society as was the finely crafted furniture from his workshops. However, in addition to these costly chairs and tables, which despite their severe design were elegant and well proportioned, with veneers of fine woods, the Wiener Werkstätten also made simple oak furniture that was eminently suited for mass production (Plate 185). Far from seeking contact with industry, however, the Werkstätten masters pursued an ideal of quality that could be

186

185. Josef Hoffmann. Small desk. 1905. Oak, solid and veneer, stained black with white paint rubbed into the pores. Made in the Wiener Werkstätten. Österreichisches Museum für angewandte Kunst, Vienna.
This is a version of a type of furniture that has existed since Baroque times, the bureau, but with the clear forms of the Wiener Werkstätten's early pieces. Hoffmann often made use of the technique of rubbing white paint into the open grain of oakwood.

186. Koloman Moser. Dining-room furnishings. 1904. Veneer—elm; inlay work —mother of pearl and snakewood in a boxwood field. Galerie Inge Asenbaum, Vienna. With the basically austere forms of this dining-room set, Moser was aiming at a *Gesamtkunstwerk* in home furnishings; whatever its other merits, it represents a very early rejection of the floral ornament of Art Nouveau.

187. Josef Hoffmann. Dining room, Palais ▷ Stoclet, Brussels. 1905–11. Executed by Wiener Werkstätten.

188. Josef Hoffmann. Nook with fountain ▷ in the hall of Palais Stoclet, Brussels. 1905–11.
The Palais Stoclet represents the epitome of the interiors executed by the Wiener Werkstätten. Not only the furnishings but all of the appliances were made there. This great project, on which cost set no limits, was realized under Hoffmann's leadership with the aid of the most talented Vienna designers, among them Michael Powolny, the potter, and Gustav Klimt, who painted the decorations for the dining room.

187

188

attained only if they personally designed every piece and supervised every step of its production. Despite Koloman Moser's leaving the Werkstätten in 1907, the basic geometric shapes he introduced continued to be used for a time, until about 1915, when the influence of the young Dagobert Peche (1887–1923) brought a changeover to almost expressionist forms—to the horror of critics such as Karl Kraus and Adolf Loos.

Financially, the Wiener Werkstätten, like Henri van de Velde's personal studio, were never a success. They ran into difficult times, particularly during the post-World War I years, and had to be closed in 1932. Josef Hoffmann still had many years to live.

The Vereinigte Werkstätten für Kunst und Handwerk, founded in Munich in 1898, headed by F.A.O. Krüger and with members of the caliber of Richard Riemerschmid, Bruno Paul (Plate 190), and Bernhard Pankok, were more concerned than their Viennese counterpart to develop furniture of high formal quality for a wide public. Like the Dresdener Werkstätten für Handwerkskunst, which the cabinet-maker Karl Schmidt called into being in 1899, their idea from the start was to produce good and inexpensive furniture and household goods in quantity—a goal which the Dresden group perhaps came closest to reaching. The Werkstätten für Wohnungseinrichtungen, established in Munich in 1902, merged in 1907 with the

Dresdener Werkstätten and changed its name to Deutsche Werkstätten für Hand-werkskunst; this in turn became incorporated in 1913 as Deutsche Werkstätten. The prime mover behind this studio was Richard Riemerschmid, who had already reached highly functional and organic solutions in his furniture designs of 1900 without any sacrifice in artistic quality (Plates 192, 193). Just as in Vienna, the men who provided the money (including Riemerschmid himself) had to jump in again and again to prevent bankruptcy. The Deutsche Werkstätten moved in 1909 to Dresden-Hellerau, where a garden city grew up around them according to plans by various architects, among them Riemerschmid and Heinrich Tessenow (1876–1950, Plate 189). Like the entire housing project, the offices and workshops themselves were superbly designed in every detail. Mass production of what was called "machine furniture" commenced in 1906. Made in solid wood according to pro-totypes designed expressly for the machine in 1902 by Riemerschmid (Plate 191) and Karl Schmidt, this furniture promised to be a great success.

From 1896 to 1903 the architect Hermann Muthesius (1861–1927) was Cultural Attaché at the German Embassy in London, where he devoted himself to the study of contemporary English architecture, especially houses, and the situation of the applied arts in general. In a number of books which aroused great interest in Germany, he advocated "...functional, practical, and up-to-date design" (Plates 194, 196). In his opinion Europe was no longer involved "...in an arts-and-crafts movement as such, but in a redesign of all forms of human expression.... Human creation is indivisible.... The same creative tendencies reappear in the work of the artisan, the architect, the engineer, the toolmaker, the tailor, the dressmaker...." In 1907 the Deutscher Werkbund was founded, largely thanks to Muthesius's efforts. Its goal, as he saw it, was to improve the level of commercial production by the mutual effort of men from the arts, the crafts, industry, and trade. At the Arts and Crafts Exhibition in Dresden in 1907 (out of which the Werkbund came), machine-made products, from furniture to stoves and railroad cars were exhibited alongside handcrafted objects of all kinds.

The work of the Deutscher Werkbund had a tremendous influence on European design. In 1910 the Österreichischer and in 1913 the Schweizerischer Werkbund were founded, followed in 1915 by the Design and Industries Association in

189. Heinrich Tessenow. Design for a bed-room. c. 1908.
The simple designs of Tessenow formed the basis for practical and decent home furnish-ings for the working population.

189

192. Richard Riemerschmid. Bay window ▷ in the living room of the Arthur Riemer-schmid House, Pasing, Munich. 1909.
Riemerschmid's greatest achievement was his attempt to lend his designs the simplicity of the English furnishings of the time.
Muthesius's description of the English house may have influenced Riemerschmid: "English homeowners want peace and quiet in their homes. Cleanliness and comfort—that is the main thing. A minimum of 'forms' and a maximum of quiet, cozy and yet fresh atmosphere...."[27]

190   191

190. Bruno Paul. Drawing of a chair. c. 1900. Archive of Vereinigte Werkstätten für Kunst und Handwerk, Munich.
A design done at about the same time as Paul's trophy room for the Paris World Exhibition of 1900. While in the latter the chairs definitely belong to the Art Nouveau canon, Paul attempted in this design to re-vive some of the forms of Empire.

191. Richard Riemerschmid. Machine-made chair (ostensibly the first). 1906 or after. Die Neue Sammlung, Munich.
A notable attempt to solve the problem of art and industry that was discussed so heatedly in the guilds and studios of the time. Its industrial character by no means reduces the comfort of this chair.

192

England, with goals very similar to those of the original German organization.

One high point in the history of the Deutscher Werkbund was its exhibition in 1914 in Cologne (Plates 195–198). This exhibition was particularly interesting in light of the controversy that arose there between Muthesius and van de Velde concerning the standardization of furniture (*Typenmöbel*). The outbreak of World War I robbed this exhibition of the success it deserved.

After the war the group resumed its activities, which led to the 1927 exhibition at

193

193. Richard Riemerschmid. Drawing of chairs for the Paris World Exhibition, 1900. Städtische Galerie, Munich, Riemerschmid Bequest.

These chairs by Riemerschmid, which in a sense presaged Danish designs of the early postwar period, were widely distributed—by Liberty in London, among others.

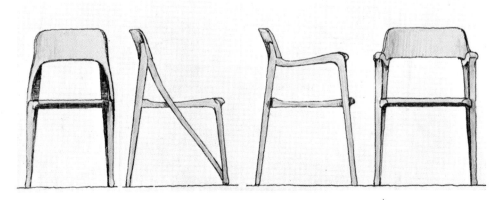

Weissenhof in Stuttgart entitled "Die Wohnung" (Plates 26, 199, 200). On the invitation of Mies van der Rohe, then vice-president of the Werkbund, leading European architects submitted their ideas on the design and construction of modern housing to this show. The buildings that resulted, the last mutual achievement of the pioneers of modern architecture, had a profound influence on the interiors and furniture design of the 1930s.

The Vienna School in the Interwar Period

The heyday of the Vienna School, led by Otto Wagner, Adolf Loos, and the Wiener Werkstätten, was a time of positive ideas and fruitful controversy that was brought to an abrupt end by the outbreak of World War I. Wagner died in 1918; Loos went to Paris; the Werkstätten, hard hit by the inflation that followed the fall of the Austro-Hungarian Empire, eventually succumbed to the crisis of the interwar years. Vien-

194

195. Karl Arnold. Caricature of the Werkbund Exhibition, Cologne, 1914. From *Simplicissimus*.
The caption reads: "Van de Velde created the individual chair; Muthesius the standardized one; and Cabinetmaker Heese the chair for sitting on." An irreverent comment on the important discussion that was then going on about the question of standardization of furniture and the place of the artist in society.
An excerpt from Muthesius's guidelines: "Architecture and with it the entire field in which the Werkbund is working cries out for standardization. Only through standardization can they regain that general significance that characterized them in ages when harmonious culture reigned."

To which Henri van de Velde replied: "As long as there are artists in the Werkbund, and as long as they still have an influence on its doings, they will protest against every attempt to form a canon or introduce standardization. The artist is by his very nature a flaming individualist, a free, spontaneous creator. . . . ."

196. Hermann Muthesius. Combination wardrobe for bedroom or dressing room. (Top part for the man, bottom part for the lady.) Drawing from the book *Wie baue ich mein Haus*.
An attempt to design really practical furniture, with detailed suggestions for its use. Muthesius gives special emphasis to the advantages of walk-in closets.

194. Hermann Muthesius. Niche with hearth under a stairway. Drawing from the book *Wie baue ich mein Haus*.[28]
Muthesius's drawings reveal much English influence—a preference he had in common with Adolf Loos. Fireplace niches (with low ceilings and benches) are often found in Loos interiors. Muthesius's book was meant as a guide for builders and homeowners, and was prefaced by a quotation from Goethe: "Though one may always make mistakes, one should never build any."

195

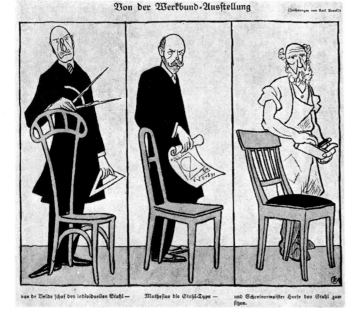

196

197

198

197. Walter Gropius. Sleeping-car interior, Werkbund Exhibition, Cologne, 1914.
Design of sleeping-car compartments (which, in contrast to American Pullman cars, were extremely private areas) gave architects the opportunity to create practical and versatile furniture for limited spaces—basically an early task of industrial design.

198. Walter Gropius. Roof garden and restaurant of the office building, Werkbund Exhibition, Cologne, 1914.
In planning for industry and administration, too, it was considered the architect's responsibility to create a more human atmosphere and better working conditions. Suggestions such as this restaurant in an office building are good examples of this.

199. Ludwig Hilberseimer. Small dining room with opening to the kitchen for serving, Werkbund Exhibition, Weissenhof Project, Stuttgart, 1927.

200. Hans Poelzig. Bedroom, Werkbund Exhibition, Weissenhof Project, Stuttgart. 1927.
Many leading architects who were not involved in the design of the buildings themselves contributed interiors and furnishings for them. Very often they used commercially available furniture, as for example Ludwig Hilbersheimer did, with the Thonet chairs of his dining room. Sometimes, however, as in the bedroom by Hans Poelzig, forms appear that were the forerunners of the modernistic, "streamlined" furniture of the thirties.

199

200

na's renowned furniture factories, which had supplied the middle class and aristocracy of the entire Balkan area with exquisitely crafted furniture, saw themselves suddenly cut off from their clients. Nevertheless, the Vienna School held tenaciously to Otto Wagner's teachings, and was inspired during the years following the war by the remarkable achievements of Josef Hoffmann, Josef Frank (1885–1967), and Oskar Strnad (1879–1935), all of whom taught at the School of Arts and Crafts in Vienna.

The architects who worked during these troubled times, among them Wagner's superbly trained students, usually had to limit themselves to furnishing apartments or shops, if they were not employed on one or another of the city of Vienna's large low-cost housing projects. The luxury furniture of the *fin de siecle* had to be brought into line with a much less prosperous world. Into the imposing apartment buildings of past epochs, many of them erected at the same time as the famous imperial Ringstrasse, came modest furnishings in a tradition reminiscent of Biedermeier. Then, as now, furniture was simple but well proportioned, and in complete harmony with its surroundings. Though these qualities were a sign of the times and by no means always voluntary, they fitted well into the new social order and the new architecture that had begun to emerge. One thing that was completely absent in Vienna, though, was revolutionary élan of the Bauhaus persuasion.

The architects of the Wiener Werkstätten, the group around Oskar Strnad, and also

201. Oskar Strnad. Desk for the living room of an architect. c. 1930.
Here great value is placed on the careful modeling of the details of this light writing desk.

202. "Haus und Garten" furniture store: three occasional tables with different basic forms. c. 1930.
Erich Boltenstern writes in the foreword of the book *Wiener Möbel*, which he edited: "Today's Vienna furniture of the type shown in our illustrations is unthinkable without the great tradition of Austrian furnituremaking, and can be fully understood only when one realizes what past epochs it springs from."[29]

202

the excellent home-furnishings establishment Haus und Garten, for which Josef Frank and Oscar Wlach worked, all designed apartments which soon had achieved quick popularity due to the many articles written about them in design magazines, particularly in Germany (Plates 201, 202). Their ideas were much imitated, but the Depression precluded the mass production of their furniture. Even the Thonet company had to agree to a merger and submit to outside management, to become Thonet-Mundus. The furniture designers of the interwar period continued to cooperate closely with architects and cabinetmakers; every detail of their products carried the mark of painstaking design and craftsmanship.

A special place among Viennese architects of the day was held by Ernst Anton Plischke (born in 1903), who had been a student of Behrens. He emigrated to New Zealand in the mid-thirties, then returned to teach at the Vienna School of Arts and Crafts after the Second World War. In him Austria had a representative of the new purist direction in architecture; his work is traceable more to the Bauhaus and perhaps even Japanese formal thinking than to traditional sources (Plates 205, 206). With his formally rigorous furniture he came the closest of any Vienna designer to the International Style of the thirties.

205. Ernst Anton Plischke. Bed-sitting ▷ room. 1933. Furniture walnut, floor covering gray, bedspread apricot-colored, upholstery beige and brown.
This small city apartment resulted from the division of a larger apartment of prewar dimensions. The clarity—and austerity—of the furniture are quite atypical for apartments of this period in Vienna.

206. Ernst Anton Plischke. Furniture in the ▷ studio of the summer house of an artist, on the Attersee. 1933–34.
This studio, whose band of windows gives a panorama of the lake, is almost an embodiment of the concept "summer house." The sparse furnishings and the visible supports of the wood construction are reminiscent of Japanese dwellings.

203. Josef Frank. Desk. Before 1926. Pyramid-grain mahogany, solid and veneer, top with leather writing surface.
A piece that in quality and precise execution of details—the upper drawers and desk top are recessed, and the veneer carried around the solid corners of the drawer fronts—is a prime example of the best in Vienna craftsmanship.

204. Josef Frank. Tea salon, installed in the Österreichisches Museum für Kunst und Industrie, Werkbund Exhibition, Vienna, 1930.
Frank, who was also responsible for the Werkbund Project of 1932 in Vienna (an attempt similar to the Weissenhof Project in Stuttgart, with about sixty buildings by Austrian and foreign architects), tried here to give bentwood chairs a new aspect by painting them and arranging them in graceful groups. Furniture painted in light colors was typical of Vienna during the thirties.

204

If we compare the Viennese furniture of this period to early forms in Sweden or Denmark, some astounding parallels come to light. Love of detail and highly skilled craftsmanship led in all three countries to very similar results—cabinetmakers' furniture that is light, elegant, and wonderfully undogmatic. This may be one reason why Josef Frank (Plates 203, 204), one of the best Viennese architects, emigrated to Sweden, where, in cooperation with the Svenska Tenn company, he put the design experience he had gained in Vienna into practice.

With World War II the Neoclassicism that had appeared here and there during the preceding decade was made the official style of Fascist governments, and the cooperation between architects-cum-furniture designers and the excellent craftsmen and factories with their skilled personnel came to an end. With it ended an important chapter in furniture history.

205

206

From De Stijl to the International Style

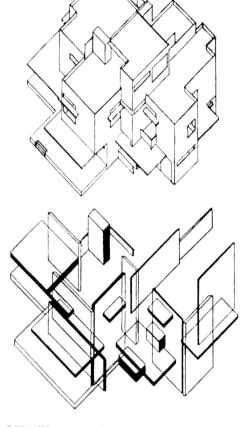

De Stijl Furniture—Theory Become Concrete

About 1917 a number of painters, architects, and writers came together in the Dutch city of Leiden, formed a group which they called De Stijl, and decided that their goal was to be nothing less than a "radical renewal of art." Their first step was to apply the Neoplasticism that Piet Mondrian and Theo van Doesburg had worked out in painting—a clear, geometric ordering of space that had its roots in Cubism—to other fields of art and to architecture. De Stijl's motto became The New Design.

Its buildings were invariably based on the cube. The group did not consider the dividing up of interior space by autonomous planes arranged at right angles to each other as a static system, but as a principle capable of infinite extension (Plate 207). Thus, to their way of thinking, buildings were an integral part of the environment for which they were conceived. With Mondrian's example in mind, De Stijl architects made use of only the three primary colors—red, yellow, and blue—with white, black, and gray for contrast if absolutely necessary. The few interiors actually finished by members of the group—such as the Aubette café by Doesburg, or his cinema in Strasbourg (Plate 208), or Rietveld's Schröder House in Utrecht (Plates 209, 210)—all held quite rigorously to this principle.

Theo van Doesburg (1883–1931) summed up the group's approach in an article of 1929: "Instead of repeating what had already been found, we wanted to take architecture and painting to heights scarcely imaginable before and to integrate them with one another as closely as possible. The house was taken apart, divided up into its plastic elements. The static axis of the old construction was destroyed; the house became an object that can be circled around from all sides. This analytic method led to new construction possibilities and to a new floor plan. The house was freed from the ground, and the roof became a roof terrace, a story opened up to the outside. At that time these problems were completely new, and nobody tackled them so seriously as the young Dutch architects and painters."[30]

The furniture designs of Gerrit Thomas Rietveld (1888–1964) are so new in terms of construction technique that they have almost nothing in common with traditional cabinetmaking—so much so that, with their radical shapes and color schemes, they really must be called concrete manifestos (Plates 209–215). Like De Stijl interiors, they are certainly not "limited" or "stable"—two words of particular opprobrium to the group. Many of the features of this furniture seem to owe much to Japanese conceptions of space, particularly in the Europeanized versions of it prepared by men like Godwin.

Doesburg's analysis of Rietveld's furniture runs as follows:

Through its new form this furniture answers the question as to how far sculpture will play a role in modern interiors. Our chairs, tables, and wardrobes, and other practical objects are the "abstract-real" sculptures of our future interiors. With respect to their construction Rietveld wrote us the following lines: "We have attempted with this chair to make every part very

207. Theo van Doesburg and Cor van Eesteren. Studies for a house. 1923. Construction and spatial principles on which De Stijl theory of architecture was based owed as much to Cubism as to the buildings of Frank Lloyd Wright. The drawing below shows an attempt to integrate interior and exterior space. In practice, the idea was not quite so successful (drawing above), with only the projecting roofs and the walls, emphasized with areas of color, fulfilling the demands of theory.

208. Theo van Doesburg. "Aubette" café and cinema, Strasbourg. 1927 (destroyed)

209. Gerrit Thomas Rietveld. Upper floor
of the Schröder House, Utrecht. 1924 .
With the design of the Schröder House,
Rietveld succeeded in creating the first truly
variable room—the upper floor, open on all
sides and visually integrating garden and
interior, can be divided by portable parti-
tions into four individual rooms.

210. Gerrit Thomas Rietveld. Corner on
the upper floor of the Schröder House, with
his "Zigzag" chairs. 1934. Photograph
taken in 1964.
In the course of time (over forty-five years),
the furnishings of this house and the use of
space changed and with the changing living
patterns of its inhabitants, an indication of
how flexible the principles of De Stijl really
were. Rietveld's "Zigzag" chair was the
only design of his to be produced in numbers
of up to about twenty.

simple, in other words to choose a primary shape that conforms to the kind of function and the material used, and in a form that is best suited to produce harmony. The construction serves to join the single parts to one another without distorting them in the least, and in such a manner that no one part overlaps the next to any great extent, or is subordinate to the next. In this way the whole stands free in space. Form has resulted from material.''[31]

211

Though De Stijl furniture designs were dictated by largely aesthetic considerations, many of them could have been reproduced by machine with no difficulty. Indeed, a number of Rietveld's later pieces were made in limited series—for instance, his "crate furniture" of 1934 (Plates 211, 212), which was sold in kit form to be assembled by the purchaser at home. Rietveld's "Zigzag" chair (Plate 210), designed expressly for mass production, was often copied and is on the market again as this is written.

Van Doesburg's untiring theoretic and journalistic activity, the numerous lectures he gave, and the exhibitions he organized, together with the few De Stijl designs actually realized, had a great influence on the postwar generation of European architects—a generation particularly open to new ideas. The formative years of the Bauhaus, for example, are unthinkable without The New Design, without Mondrian and van Doesburg, just as the young Marcel Breuer owed a great debt to the work of Rietveld. The same is true of another architect who designed highly practical furniture in De Stijl vein, the Vienna-born Rudolf M. Schindler (1887–1953). The simple, clean-lined, and inexpensive furnishings of his California houses of the thirties deserve much more attention than they have received.

De Stijl's conception of interior space—cubic rooms whose walls served not to separate but to articulate space—later became an elementary principle of the International Style. This fact shows how powerful a theory, a written manifesto, can be; though only a handful of concrete examples ever came of it, it has remained highly influential to the present day.

212

213

211, 212. Gerrit Thomas Rietveld. "Crate furniture": chair and table. 1934. Oregon pine. Stedelijk Museum, Amsterdam.
Rietveld's "crate furniture," designed in 1934, consisted of prefabricated parts to be assembled by the purchaser—an early, extremely practical, and probably cheap forerunner of cash-and-carry furniture.

213. Gerrit Thomas Rietveld, seated on the first version of his "Red-Blue" chair, with the joiners who built it and his other furniture. c. 1918.
A joiner like his father, Rietveld had attended night-school classes in architecture from 1911 to 1915. When he designed the "Red-Blue" chair—probably his most famous design—he was not yet a member of the Stijl group.

214

214. Gerrit Thomas Rietveld. Sideboard.
c. 1919. Stedelijk Museum, Amsterdam.
This sideboard of 1919, strongly influenced
by Godwin's furniture, represents a departure from traditional, closed wooden construction. The box shape has been reduced
to its separate elements.

215. Gerrit Thomas Rietveld. "Red-Blue"
chair. 1918. Die Neue Sammlung, Munich.
Frau Schröder wrote about this chair (in a
letter to Rietveld): "But as a piece of furniture a chair has other purposes than to look or
be comfortable or 'not uncomfortable.' It,
like other furniture, should contribute to
making the space in a room tangible, to
creating interior space—interior design as
sense perception of space, color, etc. . . ."[32]

215

The Bauhaus—Synthesis of Art, Craftsmanship, and Industry

The Grand Duke of Saxony School of Arts and Crafts, founded by Henri van de Velde in 1906 and devoted to the ideas of Ruskin and Morris, merged in 1919 with the School of Fine Arts of the same name to form the State Bauhaus at Weimar. Under the leadership of Walter Gropius this school was destined to become the greatest in the twentieth century for the development of modern architecture and design.

In order to understand the early Bauhaus years, one must try to imagine the situation in Weimar at the close of the First World War. Henri van de Velde's School of Arts and Crafts had been closed down in 1916 to be used as a military hospital, and all its equipment had been sold. When the new staff moved into the buildings after the war, they were faced with empty workshops; classes began to get slowly under way in 1921–22. These facts go a long way toward explaining why theory played such a predominant role in all questions of design during the formative years of the Bauhaus; there was simply no way of putting their ideas into practice. At first many

216

217

218. Marcel Breuer. Armchair. Student project, 1922. Wood, with seat and backrests of horsehair straps .
Breuer's first designs still show the influence of De Stijl theory and the work of Rietveld.

219. Marcel Breuer. Bed for the lady's bedroom in the Sample House at the Bauhaus Exhibition, Weimar, 1923. Lemonwood and walnut. (See also Plates 221–223)

220. Josef Albers. Conference table for the waiting room to the Office of the Director at the Bauhaus in Weimar. 1923. Light and dark oak .
Albers, who designed a number of chairs during his first years at the Bauhaus, also favored a Constructivist approach to furniture design.

different and often contradictory stylistic tendencies appeared in their work: Expressionist influence, which almost no important architect of the period was entirely free of, vied with the quietism of Far Eastern philosophy. Little by little, however, a body of teaching emerged that emphasized the political responsibility of the artist, in uniting the Constructivist ideas that had come out of revolutionary Russia with the approach of Dutch De Stijl.

The Bauhaus owed its stature and its astonishing resistance to continued attacks from conservative quarters largely to the diplomatic skill of its greatest teacher, Walter Gropius (1883–1969, Plate 216). He succeeded in molding a school—and eventually a movement—out of a very diverse collection of individualists with diverse artistic interests. His main goal, as expressed already in the merger of the two Weimar art schools, was to overcome the separation of arts and crafts. Gropius's ideal artist-craftsman was to have experience in handling materials as much as knowledge of design theory, in order to see things as a whole and to give objects a form commensurate with their materials. In keeping with this goal the Bauhaus curriculum was divided into two parallel streams, called *Werklehre* and *Formlehre*.

218

219

220

◁ 216. Walter Gropius. Office of the Director at the Bauhaus in Weimar. 1923. Desk, cherrywood with glass shelves .
The furniture and Constructivist-looking lamp were designed by Gropius himself and, like the rugs, were made by students in the Bauhaus workshops.

◁ 217. Photomontage with chairs by Marcel Breuer of 1921–25. Published in the magazine *Bauhaus,* No. 1, 1926 .
This picture appeared under the title, "We've got it better every day." The caption of the last illustration reads: "When you get right down to it, you're sitting on a springy column of air."

221

222

223

In 1925 Gropius wrote in his ''Principles of Bauhaus Production'':

The Bauhaus wishes to further the development of contemporary housing, from simple household goods to complete residences. Convinced that house and furnishings must be meaningfully related to one another, the Bauhaus will attempt by systematic, experimental work in theory and practice—in the aesthetic, technical, and economic fields—to derive the form of each object from its natural functions and the conditions of its use.... A thing is determined by its essence. In order to design it so that it functions properly—whether it is a vase, a chair, or a house—its essence must first be studied; for it shall have to serve its purpose absolutely, in other words, fulfill its practical functions, be durable, cheap, and ''beautiful.'' This research into the essence of objects, taking into full account all modern manufacturing methods, constructions, and materials, will result in forms that in their divergence from tradition will often seem unusual and surprising.... The Bauhaus will attempt... to train a new, hitherto unknown type of employee for industry and trade who has mastered both techniques and form in equal measure.... The Bauhaus believes that the opposition between industry and the trades is characterized not so much by differing tools as by division of labor in the former and unity of labor in the latter.... The trades of the past have changed; the trades of the future will enter a new unity of labor in which they will carry out the work of research for industrial production.

In late 1920 Marcel Breuer (born in 1902), who was to have a profound influence on Bauhaus furniture design, entered the school as a student. His designs initially showed the clear influence of Expressionism, De Stijl, and Constructivism; soon, however, his interest shifted to the problem of standardization in furnituremaking and, later, architecture (Plates 217–219). As early as 1922 he came out with a modular kitchen, which was a revolutionary innovation at the time. In 1924 Breuer was made head of the Furniture Department at the Bauhaus, and when the school was forced under political pressure to move to Dessau (1925–26, Plates 226–228), he was given his first real chance to put his knowledge and practical skill to the test. Experiments like the chairs for the Bauhaus auditorium, with their innovative construction (Plate 231), and the stools for the canteen of seamless steel tubing were the jumping-off points for a number of developments that soon led to full-fledged production prototypes.

221–223. Rooms from the Sample House at the Bauhaus Exhibition, Weimar, 1923.
The Sample House was built according to plans by Georg Muche. The relatively small rooms adjoining the high, central living room also had lower ceilings—an attempt to differentiate their functions of the type that Adolf Loos had recommended. The furniture, cubic in shape and often rather massive, disturbs the effect of unity.
The cubes in the nursery may be used as seats or as ''building blocks.'' The wall cupboard can be transformed into a puppet theater.
The lady's bedroom is furnished with Marcel Breuer designs (see also Plate 219).
221. View from the nursery through the dining room into the kitchen.
222. The kitchen.
223. The lady's bedroom.

224. Alma Buscher and Marcel Breuer. Nursery in Dresden. Designed in 1923, built in 1927.
The box-shaped furniture gives this children's room a certain severity, which is lessened a little by the bright colors used.

224

The "Wassily" (Plate 229), Breuer's first steel-tube chair of 1925, is constructed of nickel-plated, cold-drawn tubing made by the Mannesmann Company, with welded joints and glide runners. It is back on the market at this writing. Breuer is said to have gotten the idea to use steel tubing for furniture from his first bicycle. He wrote,

Already back then I was thinking about replacing the thick upholstery used on chair seats by stretched fabric. I also wanted a flexible, springy frame. The combination of stretched fabric and flexible frame I hoped would make the chair more comfortable to sit on and keep it from looking clumsy. I also tried to achieve a certain transparency of form and along with it an optical as well as physical lightness. In the course of my work on series manufacture and standardization I had come across polished metal surfaces—reflecting, pure lines in space— as new components of our home furnishings. In these shimmering, curving lines I saw not only symbols of modern technology but technology itself.[33]

225

225. Alma Buscher. Cupboard for toys. 1923.
The portable boxes may be used as tables, chairs, or play cars; the cupboard doors, as a puppet theater. The idea of nursery furniture with multiple uses was taken up repeatedly later.

226

227

Breuer and the Bauhaus designers were not the only inventors of steel-tube furniture, however. The idea was in the air; many people were on the lookout for a modern construction in steel to replace the bentwood chair. Very soon Mart Stam and Mies van der Rohe, both of whom were affiliated with the Bauhaus but not members as yet, came out with models similar to Breuer's. Stam (born in 1899), at an organizing conference for the coming Werkbund exhibition held in Stuttgart in 1926, described the prototype of a steel-tube chair without back legs—his ''S 34,'' the first of its kind to go into production (Plate 234). To guard against material fatigue, a second tube of smaller diameter was inserted into its legs. A few months later Mies van der Rohe presented his highly flexible ''MR'' chair at the Werkbund exhibition (Plate 235).

Furniture of steel tubing was the perfect illustration of the functionalist axiom, form follows function, and fulfilled all the requirements for mass production. The Bauhaus sought the cooperation of industry as a matter of course, and it was

226. Walter Gropius. Veranda with dining nook in the Gropius House, Dessau Bauhaus. 1925–26.
View of the garden and the duplex houses where the Bauhaus teachers lived. Steel-tube furniture and interior color scheme by Marcel Breuer.

227. Gropius House. Toilet niche in the guest room, with furniture by Marcel Breuer With the Fresco Department and Metalworking Shop (lighting fixtures), the Cabinetmaking Department at the Bauhaus was most involved in creating the furnishings for students' studio apartments and teachers' houses in accordance with the ideas of Gropius and his assistants.
''Frictionless and meaningful functioning of daily life is not a goal in itself, but only the prerequisite for achieving a maximum of personal freedom and independence'' (Walter Gropius).[34]

228

228. Walter Gropius and Bauhaus Workshops. Apartment of a Bauhaus student in the Studio House, Dessau Bauhaus. 1926.
The extremely simple basic furnishings used in the living area gave these studio apartments the look of scholars' cells.

229. Marcel Breuer. "Wassily" chair. 1925. Nickel-plated steel tubing. On the original model, seat, arm, and back were of fabric; since 1965 it has been available from Gavina under the name "Wassily" with optional leather covering.
Breuer's first steel-tube chair was developed independently of the Bauhaus workshops and manufactured by the firm Standard-Möbel, Lengyel & Co., of Berlin.

230. Josef Albers. Armchair, Model "ti 244." 1929. Bent wood, seat springs, and steel tubing; disassembled.

231. Walter Gropius. Auditorium of the Dessau Bauhaus. 1926. Chairs of steel tubing designed by Marcel Breuer; lighting fixtures from the Metalworking Shop, headed by Laszlo Moholy-Nagy.
The auditorium was used for meetings, lectures, and plays. The idea of a multifunctional room is emphasized by the seating, which gives the effect of lightness and portability.

230

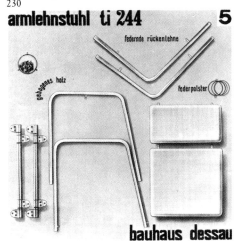

229

232. Walter Gropius. Lounge with coffee shop in the German Pavilion, International Exhibition, Paris, 1930. Commissioned by the Deutscher Werkbund.
The German contribution (book gallery with reading niches, writing desks, and a gymnasium) was designed by Walter Gropius with Marcel Breuer, Herbert Bayer, and Laszlo Moholy-Nagy. The use of steel and glass throughout created the cool, rational atmosphere of the Bauhaus style which, after it was exhibited abroad, soon spread around the world.

232

particularly important for the popularization of steel-tube furniture that, shortly after the first experimental models Breuer made for the small Lengyel Company in Berlin (this time independently of the Bauhaus—Plate 229), the giant Thonet firm took over their production. They were made in great numbers, and sold extremely successfully until 1933 and Hitler's takeover.

Breuer left the Bauhaus in 1928, working initially as an architect and interior designer in Berlin. Though his interest now began to turn more and more to architecture, he produced a number of furniture designs that pointed in new directions with their experimental use of aluminum and plywood (Plates 236, 237).

Under the supervision of Josef Albers (1888–1976), the Bauhaus "Finishing Shop" produced furniture prototypes that were meant to be both honest in construction and affordable in price (Plate 230). Work there concentrated on experiments with bentwood and folding chairs of steel tubing. Under Alfred Arndt (born in 1898), who headed the workshop until 1931, these experiments were taken even further in the direction of design anonymity. In consideration of the economic troubles of those years, Arndt believed that the primary task of his shop was to develop inexpensive furniture for manufacture by automated methods. He and his students worked out standardized parts and studied mass-production methods and ways to improve them, almost to the exclusion of the often sensational one-off designs for exhibitions that the Bauhaus workshops had produced in earlier years.

During the best years of the Bauhaus, its Interior Design Workshop had perhaps the closest working cooperation with industry of any department. Their *Entwerfer,* designers trained not only in aesthetics but in the humanities and social sciences, went straight from their apprenticeship in the school's experimental workshop to jobs in industry, and industry in turn publicized the products they designed with the help of Bauhaus advertising campaigns. The numerous exhibitions that began in 1927 lent support to this development. The Werkbund Exhibition in Stuttgart (1927), followed by the International Exhibition in Paris (1930, Plate 232) and the Bauhaus Exhibition in New York (1931), spread the cool, rational, and perhaps sometimes sterile Bauhaus style all over the world. And almost everywhere it went, it was greeted—and imitated—by the artistic avant-garde.

In 1932 the Bauhaus moved to Berlin; a year later the National Socialist authorities forced it to close its doors. Many of its teachers and students left Germany, carrying Bauhaus ideas to schools of art and architecture in other parts of Europe and in

233. Marcel Breuer. Chair without back legs. 1928. Chrome-plated steel tubing, seat and back of canework on enameled bentwood frame. Production resumed by Gavina in 1965.

234. Mart Stam. Chair without back legs, Model "S 34." 1926. Chrome-plated steel tubing.
An earlier model was equipped with canvas seat and backrest. Originally manufactured by Thonet.

235. Ludwig Mies van der Rohe. Chair without back legs, Model "MR." 1926. Chrome-plated steel tubing.
Originally manufactured by Thonet, with seat and back of canvas, which has been replaced by leather on the model produced by Knoll International since 1953.
Hans Wingler, Director of the Bauhaus Archive in Berlin, in a letter to the author on the question of who originated this chair design: "Marcel Breuer was the first to construct chairs of steel tubing, in Dessau in 1925. This new material made a reduction in mass possible. With respect to statics, however, these first steel-tube chairs were still very close to traditional wooden chairs in the sense that they rested on the ground at four points. About 1927 Mart Stam had the idea (and as far as I can tell he was the first) to use steel tubing of the diameter commonly used for gas lines to make chairs, and to bend it so that a continuous tube resulted. This enabled him to make the seat free-floating, with the frame resting on the ground not at four points but on three sides of a rectangle. The prototype of this chair by Mart Stam was shown for the first time, as far as I can

233   234   235

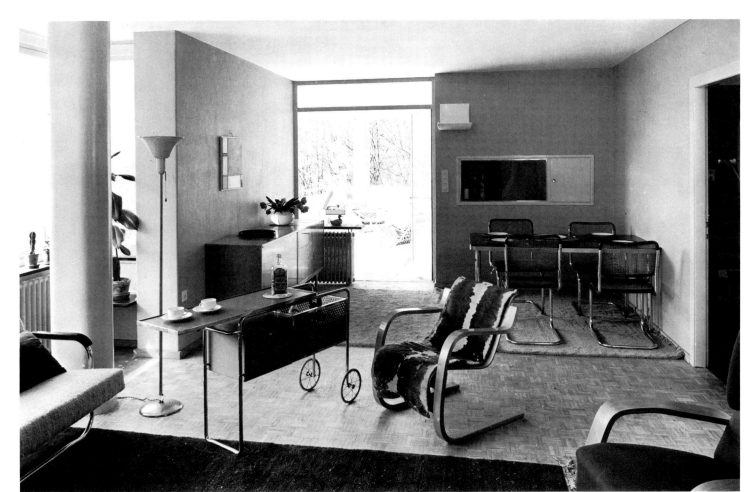

236

determine, at the Weissenhof Project in 1927. The chair or armchair under discussion, of 1928, which Thonet is manufacturing now under the name of Mart Stam, and Knoll International under that of Marcel Breuer, apparently goes back structurally, i.e. in terms of the shape of its frame, to Mart Stam's idea, while the shape and construction of the seat and backrest (bentwood and canework) are Breuer's.''

236. Marcel Breuer with Alfred and Emil Roth. Small apartment houses at Doldertal, Zurich. Living room with view onto terrace. 1934.
The combination of wood and steel furniture, and the opening of the living room onto the trapezoid-shaped terrace—whose orientation is determined by that of the buildings—provide a good example of the modifications strict Bauhaus aesthetics underwent during the thirties.

237. Marcel Breuer. Dining room, Piscator House, Berlin. 1927.
An example of the Bauhaus aesthetic as applied to every detail of an interior—sparing use of furniture, allowing the cube-shaped room to speak for itself.

America. Though the immediate social background of Weimar and Dessau which had gone so far in creating its progressive approach to design had been lost, perhaps the most valuable of its ideas, Gropius's community of architects, remained alive in the United States with The Architects' Collaborative. Mies van der Rohe's architecture, too, with its strong orientation to the requirements of modern production, found wide acceptance in the New World.

237

Furniture of the International Style—Mies van der Rohe and Le Corbusier

In the architecture of the late twenties and early thirties a new approach to building emerged, an approach that had been prefigured by Sullivan and Loos and given shape by the work of De Stijl and the Bauhaus—the International Style. This term was coined by Henry-Russell Hitchcock and Philip Johnson in 1932, in their book *The International Style: Architecture Since 1922.*[35] They wrote,

The unconscious and halting architectural developments of the nineteenth century, the confused and contradictory experimentation of the beginning of the twentieth, have been succeeded by a directed evolution. There is now a single body of discipline, fixed enough to integrate contemporary style as a reality and yet elastic enough to permit individual interpretation and to encourage general growth. . . .

There is, first, a new conception of architecture as volume rather than as mass. Secondly, regularity rather than axial symmetry serves as the chief means of ordering design. These two principles, with a third proscribing arbitrary applied decoration, mark the productions of the international style.

The social, aesthetic, and technical aspects of the International Style in architecture also characterized its interior design. The new plans and furniture prototypes developed by Walter Gropius, Marcel Breuer, Le Corbusier, Mies van der Rohe, and Alvar Aalto were to prove as important for the history of furniture as their buildings were for architecture.

Mies van der Rohe's (1886–1969) first chair design, his 1926 "MR" chair of steel tubing (Plate 235), already had a grace, elegance of line, and clarity of form that was

238. Ludwig Mies van der Rohe. Design for the Gericke House, Berlin. View from the dining room into the living area, terrace, and garden. 1930.

In this sketch it is extremely clear how Mies van der Rohe creates an active tension between furniture and interior space. The economy of means of this beautiful composition is in full agreement with his axiom, "less is more."

238

239

239. Hans Scharoun. Schminke House, Löbau, Silesia. View from the living room into the conservatory. 1932 .
Mies van der Rohe's MR chairs also fit well into the dynamic interiors of Hans Scharoun, one of the few architects to avoid the rigorously rectilinear rooms of the International Style during its ascendancy, in favor of a more expressive conception. The chairs are the first in steel tubing that Mies van der Rohe designed.

hard to surpass. A commission to design the German Pavilion for the 1929 World Exhibition at Barcelona (Plate 240) gave Mies the opportunity to realize his new conception of space in its purest form, with no concessions to utility. It was truly a work of art. Though it was taken down after the exhibition, it must be considered one of the greatest buildings yet designed in the twentieth century. In keeping with the principles of De Stijl, the pavilion had an open plan through which space flowed unhampered. The "Barcelona" chair Mies created for it (Plate 241), together with those for the Tugendhat House in Brno (Plates 242, 243), were soon acclaimed the world over for their ideal combination of clarity, harmony, use of materials, and craftsmanship.

Mies van der Rohe's furniture went into mass production after the Second World War and found many imitators. Its monumental, modern elegance has made it a standard fixture of executive suites and corporation-presidents' offices—a status symbol for our time.

Le Corbusier (1887–1965) designed very little furniture (Plates 249–252). To furnish his early houses he often chose, not lastly because of their low price, Thonet B9 chairs, wicker furniture, and sometimes even simple garden chairs and tables of iron. Some of his theoretical work done about 1922, the designs for what he called

240

241

240. Ludwig Mies van der Rohe. German Pavilion, International Exhibition, Barcelona, 1929.

Mies van der Rohe's conception of space as an element that "flows" is achieved here by freestanding walls. Exterior and interior space interpenetrate. The Constructivist look of this room is the result of the separation of load-bearing and non–load-bearing elements.

241. Ludwig Mies van der Rohe. From left to right:

Chair of the "MR" type. Canework seat and back (see also Plate 235). Manufactured by Thonet in 1926.

"Brno" chair. 1930.

"Barcelona" chair. 1929. Both "Brno" and "Barcelona" chair with frames of chrome-plated steel and leather-covered seats and backs. Both reissued by Knoll International.

Perfect balance and precision detail in connection with fine materials are characteristic of the "classic" furniture of the thirties. The originals have been back in production since the fifties—as have any number of copies.

242

242. Ludwig Mies van der Rohe. Living room, Tugendhat House, Brno. 1930.
This large room (15 x 24 m.) is divided by means of an onyx panel and a semicircular wall of ebony into four areas (entry, living, working, and dining). The large glass surfaces with their view of the garden are covered by curtains at night, and were designed to be lowered during the day for ventilation.

243. Ludwig Mies van der Rohe. Chair without back legs. Designed in 1930 for the Tugendhat House. Frame of chrome-plated steel, leather straps, and leather-covered loose cushions. Reissued by Knoll International.
With his ''floating'' construction in steel, Mies van der Rohe achieved a high degree of flexibility and versatility without the use of any type of mechanism.

243

244

244. Le Corbusier and Pierre Jeanneret. Hall of the Pavillon de l'Esprit Nouveau, Exposition Internationale des Arts Décoratifs, Paris, 1925.

"Program: *Deny arts and crafts*. But emphasize that 'architecture' runs from the smallest useful object in the home, to the street, to the city, yes, and even beyond; show that industry can produce *pure objects* by a principle of selection (series and standards); insist on the absolute value of pure works of art; point to the radical changes and new freedoms that reinforced concrete and steel have brought for the design and construction of our apartment buildings; show that an apartment can be standardized to satisfy 'mass-produced man' " (Le Corbusier).[36]

245

245. Le Corbusier and Pierre Jeanneret. Exterior of Villa Savoye, Poissy. 1929–31. The clear cube of the house (a "machine for living," an often misunderstood term) contrasts sharply with the surrounding trees; the garden interpenetrates with the interior space of the ground floor, an effect that is repeated with the roof terrace on the top floor.

246

246. Le Corbusier and Pierrre Jeanneret. Living room on the first floor with roof terrace, Villa Savoye, Poissy. 1929–31.

247

247. Le Corbusier. A house in Carthage. Living room with gallery leading to a terrace. 1928. Drawing.
Combination of one- and two-story rooms with varying heights as a continuation of Adolf Loos's conception of interior space. Furniture is used sparingly; the upholstered armchairs and couch, seemingly placed by chance more than by design, are variations on available furniture. In the right foreground a sketch of a chair with movable back of the type Le Corbusier later designed.

Immeubles-Villas—blocks of houses of several stories, which nonetheless were to retain the advantages of private homes—showed spacious rooms, the furnishings of which seem to have been left largely up to chance. The sketches show an odd mixture of futuristic, very comfortable-looking easy chairs and rectilinear, built-in furniture (Plate 247). In 1925 a design of this type was built in his Pavillon de L'Esprit Nouveau (Plate 244), a sample room for his Immeubles-Villas. Furnishings were held to a minimum, and rectilinear couch-benches were built in as modular elements; Corbusier wanted its inhabitants to live "in space" rather than "among furniture." With his chaise longue of 1928 (Plate 250), which, like Mies van der Rohe's furniture, went into series production in the fifties, Le Corbusier found a solution that not only suited the human anatomy perfectly but was aesthetically satisfying as form.

Le Corbusier's main contribution to architecture lies in his new conception of space, a conception that owes much to Adolf Loos. He was not able to put it into practice until his large villas, such as the Villa Savoye in Poissy, of 1929–31 (Plates 245, 246). The body of this house, basically cubic in form, is raised off the ground; access to its rooms and terraces is provided by ramps. Though the roof garden unites house with nature, its austere white mass contrasts sharply to the surrounding green of the landscape. The furnishings of these houses, too, often seem like foreign bodies, something added later almost as an afterthought—they are mobile, more a part of the people living temporarily in the houses than of the houses themselves.

248

248. Le Corbusier. Library in the Church House, Ville d'Avray. 1928–29. With chairs of steel tubing designed by Le Corbusier, Pierre Jeanneret, and Charlotte Perriand.
As late as the Pavillon de l'Esprit Nouveau at the Exposition Internationale des Arts Décoratifs in Paris in 1925—just as important for the further development of the International Style as Mies van der Rohe's Barcelona Pavilion—Le Corbusier was still using Thonet chairs. It was probably the steel-tube chairs shown in 1927 at the Weissenhof Project in Stuttgart that inspired him and Charlotte Perriand to make their own designs in this material.

249. Le Corbusier, Pierre Jeanneret, Charlotte Perriand. Table. 1928. Reissued by Cassina in 1965.
Top and legs are separated from each other both visually and in terms of construction —architectural ideas of the International Style as applied to furniture design.

249

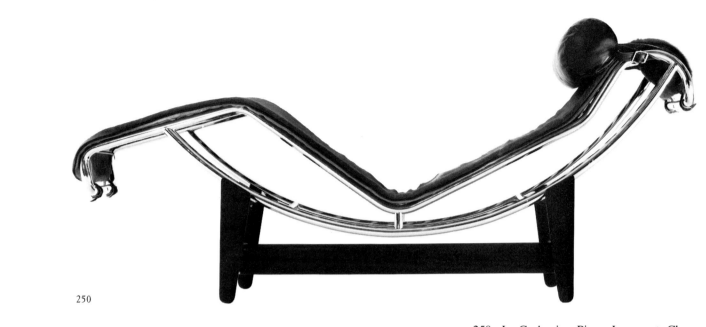

250

250. Le Corbusier, Pierre Jeanneret, Charlotte Perriand. Fully adjustable chaise longue. 1928. Lower part of frame iron, upper part nickel-plated steel tubing; upholstery horsehide or fabric. Reissued by Cassina in 1965.
The frame of steel tubing, formed to fit the human body, rests on the iron legs without being attached to them, so its position can be changed—though the user has to get up to do it.

252. Le Corbusier, Pierre Jeanneret, Charlotte Perriand. "Fauteuil grand confort." 1928. Frame nickel-plated steel tubing, leather upholstery. First manufactured by Thonet in 1929, from 1965 on by Cassina.
A chair in the shape of a perfect cube. It gives the effect of visual compactness and comes closest of any chair in formal terms to Le Corbusier's architectural language.

251

251. Le Corbusier, Pierre Jeanneret, Charlotte Perriand. Armchair with pivoting backrest. 1928. Frame chrome-plated steel tubing; armrests black leather straps; seat and back of calfhide. First manufactured by Thonet in 1929, from 1965 on by Cassina.
The back of this chair moves simply by turning on its axis—it rests on two points. With its basic cubic form and four legs, this construction contrasts sharply with the highly flexible, runner-equipped chairs of Mart Stam and Marcel Breuer.

252

Furniture for Housing Projects of the Interwar Period

Following World War I, economic depression in Germany and Austria led national and community agencies to finance a series of low-cost housing programs. Vienna, where a new Social Democratic government had taken over many of the tasks that were in private hands before the war, was one center of this activity; another was Frankfurt am Main in Germany, where Mayor Ludwig Landmann named the architect Ernst May as Head of the Board of Works (Plate 253). Strongly influenced by Dutch architecture of 1917 and after, the resulting housing projects were an attempt to combine the latest architectural thinking with the extreme restrictions on space dictated by economy. No matter how concerned their architects were to find both economic and humane solutions, the narrow stairwells of these buildings, their low ceilings, and modestly dimensioned living rooms and bedrooms precluded the use of furniture then readily available on the market.

This furniture was designed mainly for prewar, middle-class needs and simply took up too much valuable space in these public apartments. The Dessau Workshop of the Bauhaus was the only place where attempts had been made to design suitable furniture lines. The need was so pressing that in Frankfurt old furniture was dismantled and rebuilt under architects' supervision. Later the city installed woodworking machines in empty barracks and hired unemployed carpenters to build the plywood furniture that Ferdinand Kramer had submitted to a competition (Plates 255–258). Technical difficulties no longer stood in the way of mass-producing plywood furniture of this type—the construction of aircraft during World War I had provided the testing ground. This furniture was distributed by the Frankfurt Municipal Cooperative Association and sold extremely well.

In 1927, May called Franz Schuster (1892–1976) to Frankfurt to head the class in housing and interior design at the Frankfurt School of Applied Art. Schuster, who had been a student of Heinrich Tessenow in Vienna, had gained a name for himself by designing the ''Garden Suburb'' on Laaer Berg—small row houses with gardens and lawns. In addition to being in charge of furnishing the housing projects built by Ernst May (Plates 259, 260), Schuster was adviser to the Frankfurt branch of the German Home Furnishing Association, the task of which, as set out in its bylaws,

254

253

253. Ernst May and E. Kaufmann. Living room in the Praunheim Project, Frankfurt am Main. 1928. Thonet chair designed by Ferdinand Kramer for schools and kindergartens of the City of Frankfurt in 1927.
Ernst May was able to realize, from 1925 to 1930, a fine example of Social Democratic planning and social policy with this project, which became known as ''The New Frankfurt.'' For the limited space in these apartments, calculated on a subsistence-level basis, furniture had to be designed that was modest both in price and size.

254. Exhibition by the Württemberg Committee in the Municipal Housing Project at Stuttgart-Wangen. Furniture from the *Aufbaumöbel* series by Walter Gropius, 1929; chairs and armchairs by Thonet; bed and folding tables commercially available .
A remarkable attempt at combining the new box furniture with products already available on the market, to create an inexpensive but formally satisfying interior.

257. Ferdinand Kramer. Sideboard. 1926. ▷ Sold from 1928 on by Obernzenner Department Store in Frankfurt .
Kramer's article, ''Individual or Standardized Furniture,'' in which he recommended mass production of standardized products for public-housing projects, appeared in 1928 in Issue 1 of the magazine *Das neue Frankfurt.*

256. Ferdinand Kramer. Occasional tables ▷
which may be folded or extended. 1925.
Wood.
Simple shapes that are related to the furniture of the Vienna School.

256

255. Ferdinand Kramer. Desk with two drawers; stool with canework seat. 1925.

255

258. Ferdinand Kramer. Dining room of suburban house by J.J.P. Oud. "Die Wohnung" Werkbund Exhibition, Weissenhof Project, Stuttgart, 1927.
At this exhibition Kramer provided furnishings for houses by Mies van der Rohe and J.J.P. Oud.
"These buildings are not meant to look original at any cost; they use glass only to the point where a blessing becomes a liability; they have precisely that volume of living space that is feasible and desirable for working-class families. . . . That home furnishings are also on show may be mentioned in passing. For cheap mass-produced goods we can recommend only the furnishings made by the Dessau Bauhaus and perhaps those by Ferdinand Kramer of Frankfurt."[37]

257

was "to provide inexpensive, solid, and tasteful home furnishings by way of fair installment purchase to all those who find it difficult or impossible to fill their needs in any other way." In order to offer as many combinations with as few basic elements as possible, Schuster worked out his *Aufbaumöbel*, or unit furniture (Plate 23). Initially manufactured in the municipal workshops and sold via the Home Furnishing Association in furniture stores, unit furniture was later distributed by the Erwin Behr Company of Württemberg.

Schuster laid down clear guidelines for the use of his furniture in a number of exhibitions. In addition to suggested floor plans, they included designs for entire rooms, from color scheme to textiles and lighting fixtures. For the tenants of the new apartments—people who had perhaps never given a thought to design before—these shows were a guide to modern living.

Franz Schuster described his idea in these words in 1932:

258

259

The idea of *Aufbaumöbel* has spread during the past few years to all countries where furniture for the apartments in new public-housing projects is being put on the market. Unit Furniture enables the buyer to satisfy a great variety of furnishing needs with a small number of basic elements, from which he may select and add to the furnishings of his rooms at will. And it frees him from the tyranny of furniture sets, since each piece may be used for any number of different practical purposes. The night table is wide enough to serve as a shoe cabinet, a toy box for the children's playroom, or a small chest of drawers with mirror in the entry hall. The occasional table, with or without drawer or curtain, also has countless uses—it can be transformed into a folding table, for example, that is portable and does not take up valuable space in the dining room. With the chest, built-in desk, and bookcase elements you can build an almost unlimited number of combinations for living room and bedroom. This furniture

260

260. Franz Schuster. Corner in a living room of a project house, Frankfurt am Main. 1925.

"Even portable furniture can be organized more tightly by moving pieces together. In surroundings like these, which do not press in upon you, you have more freedom to live and to think for yourself—you gain in self-confidence" (Walter Müller-Wulckow).[38]

gives the apartment dweller the chance to play a creative role in designing his own home environment.

The studies conducted years later in Sweden and Denmark on optimal dimensions and norms for furniture were based largely on Schuster's pioneering work. The same may be said of the simple home furnishings produced in Germany and Austria during the immediate postwar years.

In 1925 Ernst May invited Grete Schütte-Lihotzky, a Vienna architect, to join him at the Frankfurt Board of Public Works. Here her work concentrated on the development of standardized kitchens. Her first design was shown to the public about a year later at City Hall and then installed in an apartment building in Frankfurt-Niederrad (Plate 261). When series production got under way, 4000 to 5000 such "Frankfurt Kitchens" were supplied yearly, the manufacturer even succeeding in lowering the unit price from 400 to 280 marks. This price was added to installation costs and included in the rent—making it only one mark higher per month than for apartments without kitchen facilities. The "Frankfurt Kitchen" soon set the standard for inexpensive, prefabricated kitchen furnishings in almost all countries that were concerned with public housing and its improvement.

The simple and extremely versatile furniture designed by Franz Schuster, Ferdinand Kramer's plywood chairs, and Grete Schütte-Lihotzky's prefabricated kitchens had much in common with the *Aufbaumöbel* designed by Walter Gropius (Plate 254) and the models developed at the Bauhaus under Arndt; all of them gave broad sectors of the population the chance to buy, for the first time and at very reasonable prices, furniture that was both aesthetically satisfying and could be varied according to the individual's wishes. It was popular furniture in the true sense of the word, and if post-World War II consumer society has decided to go a different path, then it is probably because there was not enough money to be made in this kind of basic design. The principle on which it was based, however, is still very much in force, if only in the design of kitchen furnishings and clothes cupboards—the principle of utility combined with versatility.

261. Grete Schütte-Lihotzky. "Frankfurt Kitchen." 1926.
Grete Schütte-Lihotzky tried to organize the components of her kitchens around the tasks to be performed, giving the highest efficiency with the least effort.

262. Grete Schütte-Lihotzky. One-room apartment of a working woman, Frankfurt am Main. 1926–27.
A separate entryway leads into a combination living and bedroom. Built-in closet (right); niche for cooking and washing on the back wall.

261

262

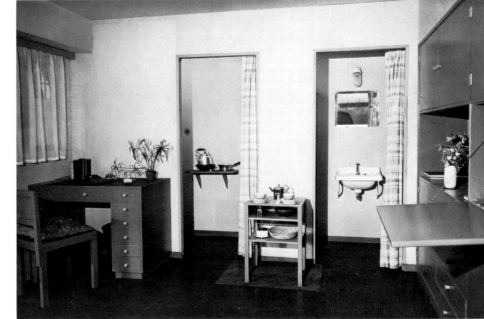

Scandinavian Furniture—from Anonymity to World Renown

Scandinavian furniture is no exception in showing parallels to developments within the societies that produced it. Sweden and Norway enjoyed long periods of peace during the nineteenth and the early twentieth century; Denmark's quarrels with her neighbors hardly affected the structure of Danish society at all. Finland, after almost five hundred years as a Swedish protectorate, became in 1809 an autonomous Grand Duchy of the Russian Empire. The struggle for political independence and national identity inspired artists to follow new paths relatively early in Finland's history, a good example of this being the National Romantic Movement at the turn of the nineteenth to the twentieth century.

263. Carl Malmsten. Cabinet. 1953. Birch with glass top.
Not only the form but the function of this piece—like many of Malmsten's other designs—is in line with the furnishing ideas of the late eighteenth- and early nineteenth-century bourgeoisie. Many of his designs were executed in his own workshops; later Malmsten even ran his own store, with large salesrooms.

All four countries had a style of living in common that was based on peasant tradition on the one hand and bourgeois civilization on the other. Their solid, comfortable furniture grew as much out of indigenous styles as English models from the eighteenth century, which, like later Neoclassical interiors, were often imitated in Scandinavia. Comparatively late industrialization and low population density certainly contributed to social stability, which meant that, in contrast to a country like Germany, no immediate need was felt to develop new forms of housing or furnishing. In the aftermath of World War II, however, when a liberal socialism combined with rapid industrialization to begin transforming social structure, people's ideas about home furnishings naturally began to change, too.

Despite the fact that the "technological" approach of the Bauhaus had taken Europe by storm during the twenties and thirties, Scandinavian designers remained true to their ideal, the furniture of the Vienna School. The conditions that had produced it could not have been more different from those in Scandinavia, however; when the wealth of the *fin de siècle* had given way to the poverty of post-World War I recession, the Wiener Werkstätten had to close down for lack of capital. Vienna's fine designers and skilled craftsmen nevertheless carried on the traditions of their great past, giving their postwar designs, modest as they were, the quiet elegance of late works. These traditions can be traced back to the Biedermeier period, and because they had been so long unbroken, the designers of Vienna rejected the revolutionary aspects of Bauhaus design for the insouciance of a carefree, mature culture.

264

In its own country the furniture of the Vienna School was only a modest success, but it soon found its way north, largely through articles in specialized German magazines. With it, the industrial forms of Thonet furniture (still known as "Vienna chairs" in Scandinavia to this day) and the work of Franz Schuster, with its emphasis on solving pressing social problems, all helped pave the way for modern furniture design in northern Europe. Alvar Aalto, the great Finnish architect and furniture designer, never tired of emphasizing how important the lectures that he heard in Helsinki as a student on the Wiener Werkstätten and Josef Hoffmann were for his later work.

Scandinavian furniture up to the fifties has one very important thing in common with Viennese furniture of the twenties and thirties, and that is the fact that both

265. Drawing from the *Möbelråd* hand-▷
book published by Svenska Slöjdförening-
en, 1961.
In addition to suggesting uses and common
quality-control methods, this handbook,
which is continually being amended, lists
about 450 quality-tested designs according
to price groups. Tests of technical quality
are on a very high level both in Sweden and
Denmark.

266. Gunnar Asplund. Werkbund Exhibition, Stockholm, 1930.
These buildings brought the formal language of the International Style to Sweden.
The strong influence of this exhibition was
felt not only in the field of architecture but
also in that of furniture design.

266

◁ 264. Josef Frank. Desk. Before 1935.
Wood painted green, compartments lined
with Macassar ebony and cherrywood.
Like Malmsten, Frank came from the
bourgeois tradition. He brought not only the
elegant proportions of the furniture of the
Vienna School to Sweden, but also, in the
color schemes of his upholstery and curtains, much of its friendly "home-and-
garden" atmosphere. Again like Malmsten,
he often used inlay work to enliven the simple rectilinear forms of his furniture.

BORDETS LÄNGD

Inte stolsbredden

**utan armbågsvidden
är måttbestämmande**

**Är bordsbenen
i vägen?**

Bordets måttsättning måste även vara sådan att
bordsbenen ej är i vägen för den sittande — inte ens
när bordet utökas.
På bilden t v är bordsbenen i vägen fastän bordsytan
är tillräcklig.

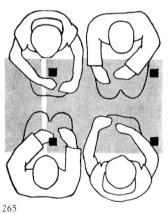 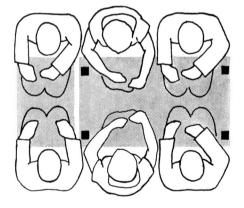

265

resulted directly from close cooperation among designers, craftsmen, and medium-
sized furniture companies. The Scandinavian countries were small and not highly
industrialized, which meant that they could afford to finish industrial products by
hand. This gave their furniture and interiors that personal quality that made them
famous after World War II—the Danish Teak Style being probably the best-known
example. Nor should we forget that Europeans had witnessed at first hand how
terribly destructive technology could be, and rather than letting cold steel and glass
into their homes they turned to traditional craftsmanship and the reassuring warmth
of natural materials. They had also had their fill of anything that smacked of
theorizing or revolution. In European design a new regionalism began to appear, and
with it a number of divergent, local styles in architecture and interior design.

Developments in Sweden

The father of modern Swedish furniture, Carl Malmsten (1888–1972), came of an upper-middle-class family; he nevertheless decided to become an artisan. His teachers, he says, were two—Mother Nature and the traditional Swedish furniture and interiors he saw in the museums. He was also influenced by the English Arts and Crafts movement, and thus considered it his duty as a designer to furnish people's homes and apartments in a way that combined utility with beauty, no matter what modern fashion might dictate. Like William Morris, Malmsten was teacher, philosopher, and artist in one. He attempted at one point to start a College of Handicrafts and Popular Art in Sweden, and up to the last years of his life he never ceased dreaming of a network of schools located outside the big cities which would provide a creative atmosphere for the combined efforts of artists and craftsmen. In a word, he mapped out the path which most Scandinavian furniture design was to follow—cultivated craftsmanship in conjunction with functional rightness, a traditional approach which nonetheless made use, even in stylistic terms, of the myriad possibilities offered by modern manufacturing methods.

Malmsten neither abandoned tradition completely nor adopted it wholeheartedly; he attempted to adapt old forms to the needs of the twentieth century. His seminal role for Swedish design came not so much from his finely balanced, craftsmanlike (and conservative) inlay work, as from the modest furniture of local fir and birch he executed, and from the many designs for series production he made. Malmsten picked up where the Neue Sachlichkeit left off. His furniture has remained unchanged for decades and is still being sold today (Plate 263).

The Stockholm Workshops held an exhibition in 1930 in which Malmsten felt he could not participate out of principle, perhaps because of the magnificent and very modern buildings of steel and glass that Gunnar Asplund provided for it (Plate 266) and which had a strong influence on younger designers. One of them, Bruno Mathsson (born in 1907, Plate 267), designed chairs which were based on detailed anatomical studies (Plates 268–272). Built first in 1933 and 1934, these chairs are still on the market. The principle on which they are based is unvarying—their separately made seats with molded wood frames rest on flexible plywood legs.

Josef Frank (1885–1967) came to Stockholm from Vienna in 1934, where he worked to the end of his life with the Svensk Tenn Company. From the "house-and-garden" atmosphere of his Vienna years he brought the playful lightness and sensuous charm of Viennese furniture to the North, combining them, however, with the discipline necessary for postwar mass production (Plate 264). The strong theoretical base of his work is certainly indebted to the ideas of the German and Austrian Werkbund.

After World War II, Sweden became the prime example of a liberal socialist country. Its high standard of living expressed itself in fine suburban apartment

267. Bruno Mathsson. Own summer house ▷ in Frösakull, Holland. 1961.
Between 1945 and 1958 Mathsson designed vacation houses of the simplest possible construction—some with wooden frames, some of concrete slabs. They all had large windows and were built without cellars.

268. Bruno Mathsson. Club chair with webbing seat and back. 1934. Footrest and reading plate designed in 1935.

269. Bruno Mathsson. The three basic forms of the Mathsson chair. 1933–35. Seat and back have a solid wood frame covered with tightly stretched webbing; lower frame is of laminated wood.

270. Bruno Mathsson. Armchair for a hospital. 1931. Solid wood with webbing.

271. Bruno Mathsson. Chair with armrests. 1942.

272. Bruno Mathsson. Study chair with high back. 1948.
"The decisive turning point in Bruno Mathsson's development came in the years 1933 and 1934. During these years he carried out his first principle and presented it[to the public]. This arose out of an investigation of the relations between chair seat, backrest, and floor. He also distanced himself from the general simplification of Functionalism. He divided the chair into an upper part, consisting of seat and back, and a lower part, consisting of the legs" (Elias Cornell).[39]

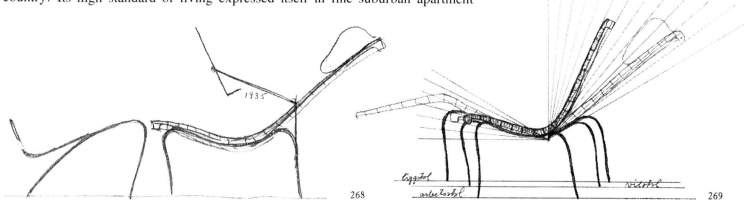

268

269

267

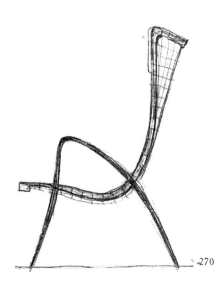

270

271

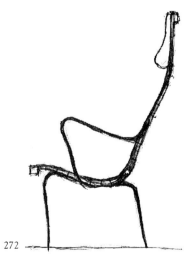

272

buildings, schools, and health-care centers. By a program of broad education, the Swedish government attempted to interest the population in contemporary styles of living, and a number of nonprofit organizations were established to manufacture and distribute inexpensive furniture without the aid of private retailers. The Swedish Consumers' Association (KF) opened its own architectural office, a consulting service for home furnishing, and its own furnituremaking shops, in addition to providing equipment for schools, laboratories, and libraries. It also published a handbook entitled *Möbelråd* (Furnishing Suggestions) that was edited by a jury of well-known architects and designers. It not only lists inexpensive and beautiful products but also gives tips on ways to use them, complete with dimensions (Plate 265). This "Home-Furnishing Bible" is written on a very high level and is truly a great aid to consumers. Then, too, home-furnishing problems are discussed with the children in Swedish schools, in the attempt to acquaint them with some of the demands of modern living.

274

Denmark's Teak Style

The architect Kaare Klint (1888–1954), who grew up in the Neoclassical tradition, was the founder of modern Danish furniture design. In 1924 he took over the new furniture class at the School of Architecture of the Copenhagen Art Academy. In addition to his enthusiasm for eighteenth-century English furniture, Klint conducted systematic studies of the theoretical principles, physiological correctness, and func-

275. Dining room, with furniture by Kaare Klint.
This modest, exquisitely crafted furniture complements even rooms of traditional proportion. Kaare Klint's school tried to create objects for the home that were both timeless and eminently practical.

276. Kaare Klint. Chair. 1936. Made by Fritz Hansens Eft.
An adaptation of the simple forms of anonymous furniture. Klint, by making

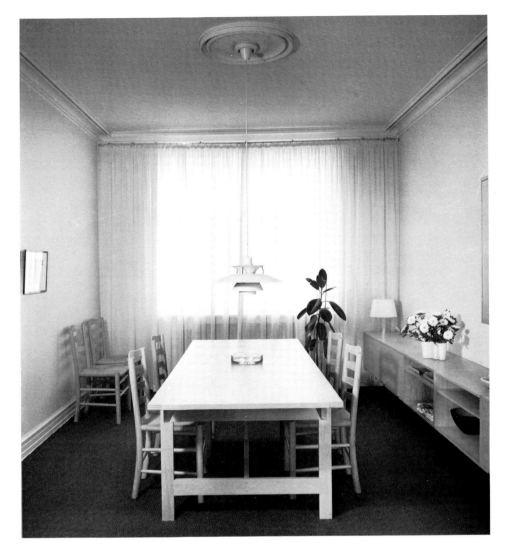

minimal changes in traditional furniture types, succeeded in adapting them to the technical and aesthetic needs of the present.

◁ 273. Knud Friis and Elmar Moltke Nielsen. Living room in a Danish one-family house. 1958. In the center a ''Safari'' chair by Kaare Klint, 1933, in solid wood with canvas or leather seat and back. Executed by Rud. Rasmussens Snedkerier.
Utility and comfort in today's small apartments have replaced the status-oriented furnishings of the turn of the century. Practical furniture, bought separately and arranged according to taste, often takes the place of complete interiors in a unified style.

◁ 274. Kaare Klint. Sideboard. 1933. Manufactured by Rud. Rasmussens Snedkerier. Klint showed a similar piece at an exhibition as early as 1926. The design is based on detailed studies of the space requirements for tableware and utensils, with the result that Klint's sideboards can hold almost twice as much as traditional cabinets.

tion of furniture. Very early on he made drawings of prefabricated furniture systems of the box type.

Klint was no revolutionary. In his work at the Art Academy he attempted to adapt a number of time-tested, earlier forms to modern furniture design, his only criteria being simplicity and fitness for purpose. He and the school he brought into being did not think of furniture in ideological terms, but attempted to reconcile traditional forms with modern function. Klint's goal was to create timeless, eminently practical furniture—what he called ''tools for living'' (Plates 273–276).

Danish furniture designers had a very important source of ideas in the annual exhibitions of the Copenhagen Cabinetmakers' Guild. the first of which was held in 1927. These shows represented an attempt on the part of Danish craftsmen to create a dialogue with their country's furniture industry, which at this time, though it was growing rapidly, was still very conservative in terms of product design. The first furniture and imaginative products they exhibited, however, were sharply criticized by the press and by many architects, who found their designs neither practical nor inexpensive enough for modern needs. Beginning in 1930, prizes were awarded before the exhibition opened for the best suggestions for new types of furniture. The prize-winning designs were then executed in cooperation with their authors; thus began the close contact among designers, architects, and craftsmen that was to prove so beneficial to Danish furniture design. A great number of the designs that are considered classic today and are on show in most of the world's museums of applied art were introduced in this way, and many of them have even gone into large-scale

280. Peter Hvidt and O. Mølgaard Nielsen. ▷
"AX" chair. 1950. Beech and mahogany
with upholstery of leather or fabric. Made
by Fritz Hansens Eft.

277. Chair by Magnus Stephensen. 1931.
Unit furniture by Fritz Schlegel. 1932.
Made by Fritz Hansens Eft.
Among the first attempts made in Denmark
to alter the traditional form of the chair;
Constructivist forms in combination with
time-tested bent wood.
The strictly rectilinear box furniture, which
was planned as unit furniture of the add-to
type, gives an early indication, especially in
its detailing, of the skill of later Danish
furniture designers.

278. Fritz Schlegel. Bentwood chair. 1930.
Made by Fritz Hansens Eft.
Like the architects of the International Style,
the pioneers of Danish furniture first went
back to the time-tested bentwood process,
whose forms had been simplified by mass
production. This chair is very similar to that
designed by Ferdinand Kramer for Thonet-Mundus for use in schools and kindergartens (1927).

279. Søren Hansen. Bentwood chair. 1930.
Made by Fritz Hansens Eft.
One of the few truly new ideas for the
bentwood process, which was stagnating in
terms of formal development.

277

278   279

280,
281. "AX" chairs and table in the hall of an adults' school, Copenhagen .
"AX" chairs were made by a process very similar to that used for the manufacture of tennis rackets—layers of beechwood glued to a mahogany core. Legs and armrests, made in one piece, were attached to the back with dowels. Seat and back, no longer necessary in terms of construction, consist of padding covered with leather or fabric. The chair is shipped in disassembled form.

production. Encouraged by the success of the Cabinetmakers' Guild, the furniture industry followed suit, opening its doors to the public with a series of exhibitions in the late thirties. The first interiors they showed—in a style that was soon dubbed "Pseudish"—met with merciless criticism. Yet Danish industry was to learn much from its confrontation with architects and expert opinion.

Perhaps the best way to trace the development of the Danish furniture industry is to take an example. There is no better one than the company founded by Fritz Hansen, a carpenter, in 1872. In its formative years Hansen's firm specialized in wooden ceilings and in the manufacture of frames for easy chairs in wood and iron. Their methods were typical of that era, in being tailored to produce furniture that looked as if it were handmade and expensive but could be offered at a relatively low price. After World War I the founder's son, C. E. Hansen, began experimenting with the Thonet process to manufacture bentwood parts for chairs. Fritz Schlegel (1896–1965) and Søren Hansen (born in 1905) provided suitable designs which, after a few abortive attempts, went into production (Plates 278, 279). In 1934 Hansen bought sole Danish rights for the manufacture of Thonet steel-tubing furniture, but a Danish court decided that the models in question did not possess enough "artistic qualities" to warrant protection by copyright. Schlegel and Hansen went on to develop unit furniture of the type introduced by Franz Schuster and the Bauhaus. After showing it at an exhibition in 1932 under the title Den Permanente, they put it on the market (Plate 277). It is a good example of the extent to which young Danish industry of the time still depended on imported ideas.

In 1950 Hansen came out with a completely new construction, which was the product of years of work with the architects Peter Hvidt (born in 1916) and O. Mølgaard Nielsen (born in 1907). Their "AX" chair (Plates 280, 281) was made of

282

283

282. Arne Jacobsen. Three-legged stacking chair. 1952. Molded beech plywood, natural color or painted. Made by Fritz Hansens Eft.
Probably the first Danish chair designed expressly with the needs of mass production in mind. The cutouts in the back increase the natural flexibility of the plywood in that area. Rubber dampers used to connect the steel legs to the seat also enhance the chair's flexibility. One-piece seat and back consists of nine laminated layers (the seven inner ones are beech, the two outer teak, oak, or maple), which are steamed, molded at a high temperature, and bonded with heat-resistant cement.

283. Arne Jacobsen. Dining-furniture group. 1957. Made by Fritz Hansens Eft.
A further development of a tested form, this time with wooden legs; stability is achieved by the star-shaped cross section of the chair legs.

laminated wood—beech on a mahogany core—a process borrowed from tennis rackets. In 1952 Arne Jacobsen (1902–1971, Plates 282–285) brought out his famous three-legged chair, with its seat and back made of one piece of molded plywood and steel legs—a design that was to become one of the most successful in Hansen's line during the postwar years. One of the main reasons for the company's growth was its consistent design policy, which was based on close cooperation between designers and technicians.

The architect Børge Mogensen (born in 1914) was for several years head of the furniture factory run by the Danish Consumers' Cooperative (FDB Møbler). Here he was able to develop inexpensive and practical furniture based on a system of dimensions he devised himself. There is no doubt that he, like Schlegel and Hansen, was inspired in this by the experiments of Franz Schuster and his circle and by the Bauhaus. Mogensen's formal discipline and mastery of materials stand in a direct line with the teachings of Kaare Klint (Plates 286–289).

The second current that contributed to the formation and success of Danish furniture stood in opposition to the austerity of the International Style. Its representatives favored the strongly modeled, sculptural forms that for a long time were considered typical of Danish design.

Finn Juhl (born in 1912), who started out as an architect, had a difficult time

284

284. Arne Jacobsen. "Egg" chair. 1959. Steel base, revolving seat of plastic with foam-rubber upholstery covered with fabric or leather. Made by Fritz Hansens Eft.

285. Arne Jacobsen. "Swan" chair with footstool. 1959. Steel base, revolving seat of plastic with foam-rubber upholstery covered with fabric or leather. Made by Fritz Hansens Eft.
For his large architectural projects Jacobsen designed furniture, appliances, and textiles which often went into mass production later. He was a master at making use of all the technical and aesthetic possibilities of even new and untried materials. The difficulty in executing these designs lies in fitting the leather or fabric covering precisely to the shape of the chair shells, which have been designed for optimum comfort.

285

286

287

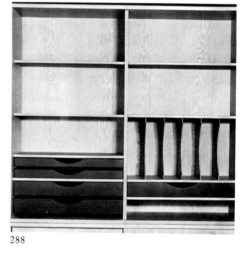

288

289

286. Børge Mogensen and Grethe Meyer. ''Boligens Byggeskabe'' cabinet elements. Shown for the first time at the Copenhagen Cabinetmakers Guild Exhibition, 1954.
This design is a result of the desire to create a piece of furniture capable of holding all of the utensils used in the home (including radio and TV equipment). In 1956 a system of dimensioning based on the normal height of Danish apartments (2.5 m.) was devised, allowing the use of either separate elements or the entire ''cabinet wall'' in integrated form.

287. Børge Mogensen. Sofa for two persons. 1945. In production since 1962.
Mogensen, who began his career as a cabinetmaker, has designed both mass-produced and handcrafted furniture.

288. Børge Mogensen. Detail of shelves from the "Øresund" series. 1955–67. Oregon pine, oak, or teak.
Other considerations led to the development of this system, which is based on elements that are 134.7 cms. wide and either 36.7 cms. or 54 cms. deep. Their heights are a multiple of the basic dimension of 19.6 cms. The elements based on this system of dimensioning are versatile—their use is not limited to the living room or kitchen.

289. Børge Mogensen. Furniture for a bedroom. 1945.
An example of Mogensen's early work that shows his love of simple, clean construction.

290. Finn Juhl. Group with "136" armchair. 1958. Teak with foam-rubber upholstery. Manufactured by France & Søn.
Typical of Juhl's chairs is their "floating seat," which usually rests on only two edges. This emphasizes their very sculptural forms, the construction as a whole playing a secondary role.

finding buyers for his organic chairs in Kaare Klint country. Not until they were successful abroad were they accepted at home. Characteristic of the designs he produced in the ten-year period between 1945 and 1955 is the way in which he dissolves the traditional armchair into its two separate and clearly defined components—the frame and the seat, which the frame is there to hold up (Plate 290). Juhl's "furniture sculptures" were featured in the Cabinetmakers' Guild Exhibitions year after year, and soon had become world-famous.

Hans J. Wegner (born in 1914) comes from a family of craftsmen. In cooperation with the cabinetmaker Johannes Hansen, he has created a series of excellent pieces that, in stylistic terms, fall somewhere between Kaare Klint's discipline of form and Finn Juhl's temperament. His designs are very amenable to mass production—so much so that five factories merged under the name Salesco to devote themselves to manufacturing Wegner's furniture (Plates 291–294).

In sum, the individual quality of Danish furniture has been largely the result of the way it is made; industrial prefabrication and hand finish give it a unique combination of utility and personal style. Danish furniture, like Swedish, is also under continual quality control to keep standards high. Each piece is subjected to stringent tests and inspections, and seals of furniture quality are awarded by a jury of experts. Advertising and distribution are also under rigorous supervision; at the Cologne Furniture Fair, for example, only those Danish firms are given permission to exhibit that hold to the high standards of their industry.

290

The great export success of Danish furniture began in the early fifties. Soon Denmark was sending over half of her total production abroad; a country without wood of its own had become a leader in furniture manufacturing. A number of talented designers—Børge Mogensen, Ole Wanscher, Hans J. Wegner, Grete Jalk (Plate 295), Arne Jacobsen, and many more—took up the challenge of form and material and created those rare syntheses of precision construction, imagination, and truth to materials that have earned Danish furniture its international reputation. Nor should it be forgotten that Danish designers have done fine work in the area of simple furniture for the limited budget.

In the last few years we have been hearing less about the type of furniture that has come to be known as "typically Danish." Arne Jacobsen, Poul Kjaerholm, and Jørn Utzon have actually always been closer to the International Style, and the young generation of furniture designers is busy trying out new materials and livelier forms; for the moment at least, it seems that the most interesting things happening in Danish design have been imported from Italy.

291

293

292

291. Hans J. Wegner. Armchair. 1949. Teak with Spanish cane. Made by Johannes Hansen.

292. Hans J. Wegner. Folding chair. 1949. Oak with Spanish cane. Made by Johannes Hansen.
Both chairs are characterized by extreme simplification and logical formal and constructive articulation in the tradition of Kaare Klint.

293. Hans J. Wegner. Table and three-legged chairs. 1953. Oak and teak. Manufactured by Fritz Hansens Eft.
A stacking chair that, with its extremely simplified form, is particularly well-suited for auditoriums. Its small size is also an advantage in the dining nooks of today's tiny apartments.

294

294. Hans J. Wegner. Group of furniture in a vacation house with ''Y chair.'' 1950. Untreated or painted oak. Made by Fritz Hansens Eft .
Further development of a chair type that goes back to Chinese models of the eighteenth century.

295. Grete Jalk. Chair. 1963. Molded laminated wood (oak). Made by P. Jeppesen. This series consists of stools, chairs, tables, and table sets. Its construction makes full use of the possibilities of laminated wood. Its sculptural articulation leads out of the Danish style into furniture forms that could be easily manufactured in modern plastics.

295

Alvar Aalto—Fantasy and Construction in Wood

The dialogue that took place between Finnish craftsmen and artists of the Historical Revival at the turn of the century came at a time of turmoil—Finland's battle for political independence. And as so often in history, artists answered the attempt to suppress a national movement by returning to indigenous traditions. The peasant culture of their country, which had been annexed to Sweden for almost five hundred years, began to exert a great fascination on young Finnish craftsmen. This, together with the influence of the Arts and Crafts movement and Jugendstil, brought about the flowering of a new Finnish style in the applied arts. It became known as National Romanticism, and its golden age was the first decades of the twentieth century.

The painter Akseli Gallén-Kallela (1865–1931, Plate 296), who illustrated the Finnish national epic, the *Kalevala,* with a cycle of paintings, was one of this movement's greatest representatives. His Swedish friend, Louis Sparre (1886–1964), with whom he had hiked through vast areas of Karelia in search of simple peasant furnishings, established the Iris Company in 1897 at Porvoo, and with it modern Finnish furniture design. Sparre, who had already designed furniture in the National Romantic style, was an advocate of William Morris and had acquainted himself with almost all European design tendencies on his long travels. When he opened his new company's doors, Sparre made a point of emphasizing that its production was not going to be determined by "material profit interests." Sparre's formal ideas owed much to English and Austrian models (Plates 297, 298).

In 1896, three young architects, Herman Gesellius (1874–1916), Armas Eliel Lindgren (1874–1929), and Eliel Saarinen (1873–1950),came together to form a cooperative. Contest prizes and a commission to build the Finnish pavilion at the Paris World Exhibition of 1900 enabled them to put up a large studio with living quarters on the outskirts of Helsinki, an imposing edifice of granite and wood in the National Romantic style. Called "Hvitträsk," this building (Plate 299), with its many rooms radiating out from a barnlike hall, was a prime example of that type of turn-of-the-century interior design that gave craftsmen an absolutely free hand.

297

296

296. Akseli Gallén-Kallela. Chair. c. 1900. Birch with handwoven woolen upholstery (pine motif in green on blue background). Museum für Kunst und Gewerbe, Hamburg .
The simple shape of this chair may be traced back to Biedermeier; it emphasizes the combination of craftsmanship and folk art.

297. Louis Sparre. Chair, from Louis Sparre's study. 1902–33. Leather seat and table of mahogany .
Sparre, who designed dining-room furniture in the Finnish style as early as 1894, was particularly taken by the furniture and textiles he saw at Liberty & Co. when he visited London in 1896. The rigorous and muscular forms of his furniture stood in sharp contrast to most Continental Art Nouveau.

298. Louis Sparre. Sofa. 1906. Pine stained dark brown .
In this simple piece Sparre's love of sturdy forms is particularly in evidence.

298

299

300

299. Herman Gesellius, Armas Eliel Lindgren, Eliel Saarinen. Living room of the "Hvitträsk" studio and residence, Kirkkonummi. 1902 .
Hvitträsk, designed by architects to work and live in, was built in the untouched Finnish countryside. Although influenced by Art Nouveau in its details, its log architecture is almost medieval in character, making it a typical example of Finnish National Romanticism.

300. Eliel Saarinen. Desk with revolving chair. c. 1907. Oak with inlays of reddish flowers on a greenish background .
National Romanticism and international influence, here perhaps on the part of the Wiener Werkstätten, balance each other in the design of this furniture with its heavy, cubic forms.

301

302

Alvar Aalto (1898–1976) and a group of young architects worked for Saarinen at "Hvitträsk." Aalto's academic training had been in Classicism, but he also attended lectures on Josef Hoffmann and the Wiener Werkstätten. After the First World War he turned to the ideas of the New Architecture and himself contributed a great deal to the formation of the International Style; however, again and again in the course of his career he went back to elements distilled from Finland's national tradition.

In 1928 Aalto and his wife Aino won the competition for the Paimio sanatorium, for which he also designed his first furniture (Plate 308). Since one of Aalto's main tenets was that the human body should come into contact only with organic material, he opened an experimental workshop in a local woodworking firm to try out various means of molding wood (Plates 303, 304). His most original idea was to make use of the natural moisture in woods such as birch, which he came to prefer to all others, rather than bending it by steaming alone, as in the Thonet process. His first chairs with molded plywood seats (Plate 302) were flexible and very comfortable; they had legs of steel tubing, which on later models were replaced by laminated wood. At about the same time as his experiments at Paimio, in 1930, Aalto exhibited his first stackable chairs at the Helsinki Arts and Crafts Exhibition in a model room called "The Minimal Apartment" (Plate 301).

301. Alvar Aalto. Living room for the exhibition "The Minimal Apartment." 1930. For the first time in its fifty-year history the Helsinki Exhibition of Applied Arts held a special show in 1930 dealing with the problems of public housing and the furnishing of model apartments.

302. Alvar Aalto. Stackable chairs. 1930. Aalto made his breakthrough with his free-floating chair, which had a frame made of steel tubing. The molded plywood seat—the new element here—was connected to a frame that reminds one of the designs of Marcel Breuer and Mart Stam. The backrest is unsupported.

303

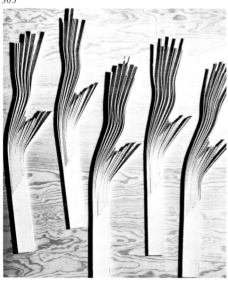

304

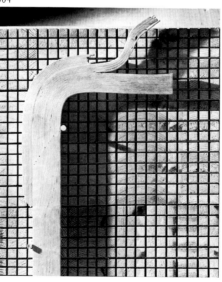

303, 304. Alvar Aalto. Experiments in wood.
"In order to reach practical goals and lasting aesthetic forms in connection with architecture, you cannot always begin from a rational and technical standpoint—perhaps even never. Man's imagination must be given free rein. That's the way it usually was with my experiments in wood. Purely playful forms, with no purpose at all, did not lead to useful forms in some cases until ten years later" (Aino and Alvar Aalto).[40]

305

305. Alvar Aalto. Discussion and lecture hall, library at Viipuri. 1930–35 .
Aalto solved two crucial problems in this library: the reading rooms receive sufficient light from newly developed round skylights ("In a library light is the primary thing"), and in the lecture hall the wave-shaped ceiling of thin wooden laths makes for excellent acoustics.

Aalto can hardly have known at this time about the American patents for laminated wood furniture of 1878, which Sigfried Giedion mentions in his book, *Mechanization Takes Command*. The same may be said of Thonet's very similar experiments (Plate 85), only a few examples of which were on view in the company museum and which had not been published anywhere. We should probably look no further for a possible inspiration for Aalto's idea than the laminated wood skis that had been in wide use in northern Europe for decades.

For the library in Viipuri (1927–35), whose wave-patterned acoustic ceiling is often cited as the first example of Aalto's "organic architecture," he designed seating that was a direct result of his Paimio experiments and in which no steel parts

306

306. Alvar Aalto. Stools and chairs for the Viipuri library. Developed 1929 to 1935. Manufactured by Artek.
The basic principle of this furniture was worked out between 1929 and 1935. The solid wood of the legs was cut through laterally at the point of bending to give it the needed flexibility. The legs are attached to the wooden seats with screws.

were used at all (Plates 305, 306). The stools are still being manufactured today. A short time later Aalto and his wife, together with Mairea Gullichsen, established the Artek Company, as "a center for contemporary furniture, home furnishings, art and industrial art"—but mainly to manufacture Aalto's furniture. Aalto referred to furniture as "accessories to architecture" and said of his experiments:

The first experiments consisted of bending laminated pieces in one direction only. It has always been my dream to create multi-dimensional, sculpture-like wooden forms that may someday lead to freer and more stable forms. The first attempts to construct organic volumes out of wood without resort to cutting or carving led later, after almost ten years, to triangular solutions that took the direction of the wood grain into account. The vertical, load-bearing element in furniture is so to speak the little sister of the column in architecture.[41]

Sigfried Giedion writes of this technique:

By a special suction process it is possible for wood to acquire such suppleness and flexibility that the architect may twist it and turn it as he pleases. Further, chemists have found a method of forming a cable-like structure from a number of small rod-like pieces of wood tapered at both ends: "Wood macaroni" Aalto calls them.[42]

About 1937 Aalto went one step further, and left off the laminated wood frames of his chairs altogether, giving them a flexible base much like that of earlier steel-tubing chairs (Plate 310). Aalto's furniture, even the mass-produced pieces, is always just as much an integral and personal part of his architecture as the lamps and doorknobs he designs. It expresses his attitude to materials and his humanistic approach to architecture. The younger generation of Finnish architects, long dominated by Aalto's strong personality and organic architecture, has returned somewhat belatedly to the International Style. In furniture design the names of Ilmari Tapiovaara (born in 1914), Antti Nurmesniemi (born in 1927), and the Asko Company deserve mention, all of whom have begun to distance themselves from the specifically Finnish element in furniture styling.

308

307. Alvar Aalto. Stool. 1954. Construction with fanned bends. Manufactured by Artek.
Bent, solid wood which again is transformed by the process of sawing into laminated wood—this time in three dimensions—and which melts into the wood of the seat. This construction, in which no screws are used, is perhaps Aalto's most beautiful and mature, the final phase of a comprehensive development.

308. Alvar Aalto. Armchair for the Paimio sanatorium. Developed 1929 to 1933. Manufactured by Artek.
During Aalto's first phase (1929–33), in which he experimented with laminated wood for seats and backs on a steel or wooden frame, he also designed chair forms in which curved seats were held by closed or open laminated wood frames. For the sanatorium in Paimio, Aalto designed light, standard chairs of wood, a material he considered better adapted to the human body than steel.

310. Alvar Aalto. Armchair. 1935–39. ▷
Bent birch; seat of various materials; the chair illustrated has fabric straps. Manufactured by Artek .
Between 1935 and 1939 Aalto designed, in addition to chairs, simple, standardized furniture such as wardrobes and bookcases, all with bases of—usually flexible—laminated wood attached to frames of the same material.

309. Karl and Eva Mang. Living room of the Haus im Waldviertel, Lower Austria. Chairs and table by Alvar Aalto. Chair 406 with red fabric straps, table with glass top. Both manufactured by Artek .

310

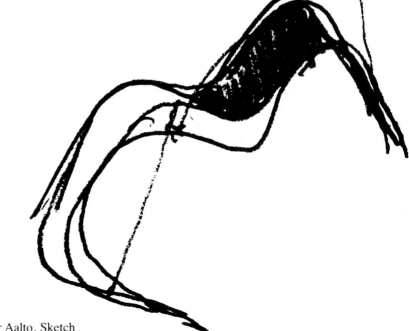

311. Alvar Aalto. Sketch .

Furniture Design After World War II

New Technologies: The United States

In the Scandinavian countries, as we have seen, many new furniture designs and manufacturing techniques were developed despite the war. In Germany, however, the great stream of the international movement that had originated there was capped at its source when Hitler came to power. The Dessau Bauhaus was closed in 1932 and moved to Berlin, where its stay was short; a few years later Walter Gropius, Marcel Breuer, Ludwig Mies van der Rohe, and many others were already in the United States. There the leading architects of the International Style found a new audience for their work, and American universities welcomed them with open arms.

The pseudo-Classicism favored by the dictatorships was not without influence on the rest of Europe; only in Italy were there signs, at least in the field of industrial design, that elements of the International Style had survived, if in a form tailored to fit Fascist ideology. By the end of the war the *völkisch* influence had not only discredited itself but brought about such large-scale destruction in Western Europe that there was no choice but to make a completely new start.

The most pressing task was to rebuild the countless homes and apartment buildings that had fallen prey to the bombs. Europe's furniture industry, or that part of it that had escaped destruction, had had neither the chance to develop new ideas nor to experiment with new materials—Fascist ideology and the priority of war production had made sure of that. It was faced by an intact and dynamic industry across the Atlantic which, with the help of important European architects and teachers, had come to play a leading role in furniture design. American technology had taken a giant step forward during the war and was quickly able to adapt to peacetime needs. War research, particularly on the use of plastics in aircraft production, soon found wide application in a number of consumer goods.

The initial step in this direction had been taken much earlier, however, with the contest sponsored by The Museum of Modern Art at the suggestion of Bloomingdale's department store in 1941, entitled "Organic Design in Home Furnishings" (Plates 312, 313). First prizes for chairs were awarded to the team of Charles Eames (1907–78) and Eero Saarinen (1910–60). The forms suggested by these two architects—three-dimensional shells—led, in their complete rejection of the right angle, out of the two-dimensional formal world of bentwood and steel chairs of the Breuer or Aalto type into a new sphere of "sculpted" furniture based on the latest technology. Most of the furniture that the Herman Miller Company was to make, in cooperation with Charles Eames up to the sixties, can be traced back to the results of this contest (Plates 314–320). It is safe to say that without the initiative of this then-unknown firm, the logical development that soon had made the United States the leading producer of modern furniture in the world would not have been possible. George Nelson (born in 1907), a designer who also worked closely with Herman Miller (Plates 321, 322), wrote the following about this enterprise in one of its catalogues:

312, 313. Charles Eames and Eero Saarinen. Chair and cabinet units. 1940. Drawings for the contest "Organic Design in Home Furnishings," The Museum of Modern Art, New York, 1941.
The first chairs and cabinets made according to these drawings by Eames and Saarinen were shown in an exhibition at The Museum of Modern Art in 1941. Production was initially held up by the war and also by the difficulty of realizing these designs in technical terms. After years of experimenting in small workshops and Eames's own studio, the improved models were taken over in 1946 by Herman Miller. "I think of myself officially as an architect. I can't help but look at the problems around us as problems of structure—and structure is architecture" (Charles Eames).[43]

314. Charles Eames. Chair. 1946. Seat and back of molded plywood and base of chrome-plated steel tubing. Manufactured by Herman Miller, Inc.
Prototypes of this chair, on which the seat and back were separated to simplify production, existed as early as 1944. A number of artists and technicians helped Eames and his wife, Ray, with their experiments. The forms of the plywood parts were developed using full-scale plaster models, which were transferred directly to the experimental molding press.

315. Charles Eames. Armchair. 1950. Metal-rod base and molded plastic seat. Manufactured by Herman Miller, Inc.
In 1948 The Museum of Modern Art in New York gave Eames a research grant to develop new types of furniture. The bucket shape of 1950 was made of metal with a layer of sprayed-on neoprene. This model was awarded second prize in the "International Competition for Low-Cost Furniture Design," sponsored by The Museum of Modern Art. Since the tooling costs were too high, Eames experimented with fiberglass-reinforced polyester, which was then used in production.

316. Charles Eames. Chair. Metal-rod base and seat of heavy formed wire, partially covered with fabric. Manufactured by Herman Miller, Inc.
An attempt to unify base and seat in terms of structure and material.

A3501

SIDE CHAIR

312

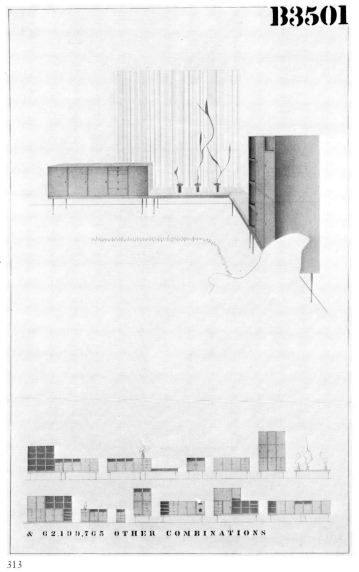

B3501

& 62.199,765 OTHER COMBINATIONS

313

314

315

316

317

318

317. Charles Eames. Table and chairs. 1944–46. Molded plywood with bases of metal rod and plywood. Manufactured by Herman Miller, Inc.
"A piece of furniture that harmonizes with a beautiful room or beautiful surroundings more or less recedes into the background. It fulfills its purpose best when it is not the primary object of attention. I feel flattered when I see that this is already true of some of my designs" (Charles Eames).[44]

318. Charles Eames. Chairs. 1958. Aluminum base, padded seat, and fabric upholstery. Manufactured by Herman Miller, Inc.
"Charles Eames has contributed at least three of the major chair designs of the twentieth century. . . . His work has influenced furniture design in virtually every country, and his mastery of advanced technology has set new standards of both design and production" (Arthur Drexler).[45]

319. Charles Eames. Chair and stool. 1957. Aluminum base, molded rosewood plywood seat and back, leather cushions with foam-rubber padding. Manufactured by Herman Miller, Inc.

Composed of many individual parts and several different materials, this lounge chair is like a modern sculpture. "Don't ask me about new lines and silhouettes. I'm more interested in utility and the way things present themselves in a room" (Eames).[46]

320. Charles Eames. Armchair. 1971. Aluminum base and padded seat shell of molded polyester with loose cushion. Manufactured by Herman Miller, Inc.

"Technically, this chair is among Eames's most sophisticated and carefully studied productions. Its plastic shell receives a formed-in-place urethane foam padding, covered, like the upholstered side chair, by a vinyl or fabric skin. Dents in this material slowly disappear, the urethane having a 'memory' for its original contours" (Arthur Drexler).[47]

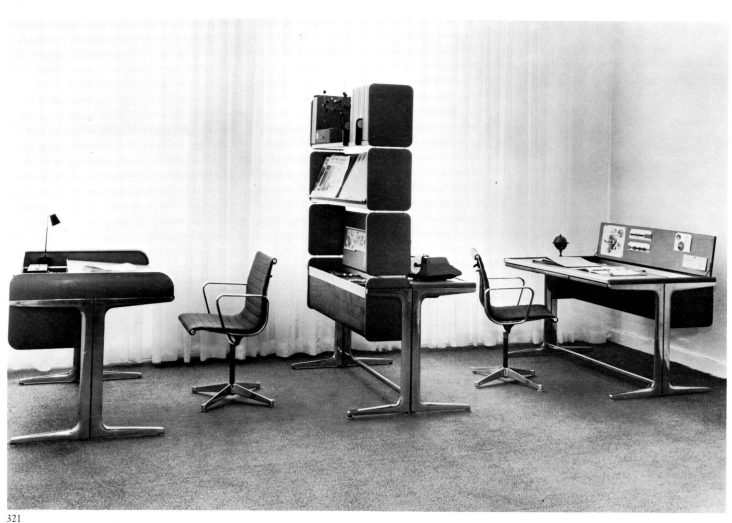

321

322. George Nelson. "Coconut" chair. 1956. Manufactured by Herman Miller, Inc. George Nelson—architect, writer, and designer—became the first Design Director at Herman Miller in 1946. This company, one of over 4000 other furniture factories, located in a small town near Grand Rapids, Michigan, was founded in 1905. By 1931 it was one of the pioneers of modern design in America.

322

◁ 321. George Nelson and Company. "Action Office" line of office furniture. 1964. Bases of polished cast aluminum, footrest chrome-plated, sides of molded plastic, writing surface of vinyl. Manufactured by Herman Miller, Inc.

323, 324. Harry Bertoia. Chair. 1952. Chrome-plated or plastic-coated steel rod, padding covered with cotton fabric or flexible artificial leather. Manufactured by Knoll International.

Harry Bertoia, who has taught painting and metal sculpture, was asked by Hans and Florence Knoll "to do what you feel like." The result was his wire chairs: "In the sculpture I am concerned primarily with space, form, and the characteristics of metal. In the chairs many functional problems have to be established first . . . but when you get right down to it, the chairs are studies in space, form, and metal too" (Harry Bertoia).[48]

324

323

It is a small company that is run by its owners themselves in a small town. What makes it different from others are the following principles:

1. *What* you do is the important thing.
2. Design is an integral part of business.
3. The product must be honest.
4. *You* decide what you want to produce.
5. There is a market for good design.

This program is aimed at introducing a standing collection; i.e., each piece will be manufactured until it no longer conforms to the situation or can no longer be improved.

Miller and his colleagues devoted much study to processes for molding plywood in three dimensions, as well as to the problem of attaching metal legs to plywood seats and molded plywood parts to one another. Particular attention was given to the use of new plastics from the aircraft-manufacturing field and to an industrial spot-welding technique for making bucket seats of metal rods. For the first time since the Thonet chair, industry had begun to take advantage of its chance to put the best experimental designs into production. Though only a handful of the Eames prototypes were ever manufactured by Miller on a large scale, they were nevertheless to prove of seminal importance for the furniture design of the next twenty years.

The great upswing in American skyscraper architecture, which came with the dissemination of Mies van der Rohe's ideas, gave another firm, Knoll Associates, the opportunity to apply the tenets of Bauhaus functionalism to the American scene. Buildings that were technically perfect cried out for perfection in furniture and interior design—a perfection that could be realized only by closer cooperation between progressive furniture manufacturers and young designers.

Eero Saarinen began working for Hans Knoll (1914–55) and Florence Knoll (born in 1917) as early as 1943 (Plates 325–328). The Knolls, who were designers themselves (Plate 329), opened branches of their firm in Germany and France in

325

325. Eero Saarinen. "Womb" chair. 1970 (designed in 1948); footstool, 1972. Bases matt-chrome steel tubing, seat molded plastic with foam-rubber padding covered with wool material. Manufactured by Knoll International.
This chair reminds one of the contest design Saarinen did with Charles Eames for The Museum of Modern Art in 1941. Saarinen wanted "a big, wide chair that you can snuggle into." Its basic element is a prefabricated plastic shell that has been reinforced with fiberglass.

326

326. Eero Saarinen. Easy chair and stool. 1948. Frame laminated birch, spring upholstery covered with foam-rubber layer and fabric. Manufactured by Knoll International. The basic principle of this chair is similar to that of Aalto and Breuer designs of the pre-World War II period, and its structure is more typical of Europe than of the United States.

327

327, 328. Eero Saarinen. Chairs and table. 1956. Cast alloy with white plastic coating, seats of pressure-molded white polyester with padding covered with fabric; table top Italian marble. Manufactured by Knoll International.

The first ideas for Saarinen's ''one-leg models'' were born in 1953. Scale models were made in one-quarter actual size and tested in a model room. ''As to the pedestal furniture, the undercarriage of chairs and tables in a typical interior makes an ugly, confusing, unrestful world. I wanted to clear up the slum of legs. I wanted to make the chair all one thing again'' (Eero Saarinen).[49]

328

329

1951, and in 1955 they began producing and distributing Mies van der Rohe's prewar furniture designs (Plate 330). As time went on they added a number of gifted designers to their lists, among them Harry Bertoia (1915–78, Plates 323, 324), and later, with the purchase of the Italian firm Gavina, Vico Magistretti, Tobia Scarpa, and others (Plate 332). With Gavina they also took over the production of Marcel Breuer's designs of the twenties and thirties.

330

329. Florence Knoll Bassett. Furnishings for the reception room, office of the Connecticut General Life Insurance Company, Bloomfield, Connecticut. Architects Skidmore, Owings & Merrill, built 1954–57.
Furniture for offices and reception rooms grew more and more elegant and luxurious during the sixties. Teak, rosewood, marble, and polished steel were typical of the "Knoll look." Florence Knoll and her planning team also performed design commissions for the interiors of large corporations. With the development of office systems, the design of printed textiles and lamps, and the introduction of an accessory department (vases, dishes, etc.), Knoll became a furnishing house of international stature.

330. Dining room, with "Brno" chairs by Mies van der Rohe and a table by Eero Saarinen. Manufactured by Knoll International.
This interior of the sixties corresponds in furnishing and spatial conception to the tenets of the International Style.

331. Robert Haussmann. Chair. 1955. Base flat-sectioned spring steel, with leather straps and loose leather cushions. Manufactured by Haussmann & Haussmann.
This chair, which is easily dismantled for transport, is based on the ideas of Mies van der Rohe. Though Mies's designs were thought through to the last detail, they were still capable of further development, as this beautiful chair shows.

The Knoll and Herman Miller companies, often pacemakers in furniture design (Plate 331), still hold a high rank in the field today. Though their immaculate chrome and leather chairs are by no means inexpensive, the growing market for prestigious furnishings for the executive suites of the sixties gave both designers and industry fine opportunities to develop and perfect a series of daring designs.

The International Style and Beyond

The International Style in architecture and design, already in its inception during the early years of the Bauhaus and given lasting form by men such as Mies van der Rohe, Marcel Breuer, and Le Corbusier, was taken to a new level of perfection in postwar America. Its pristine architecture of steel and glass had a very understandable

332. Tobia Scarpa. "Bastiano" sofa. 1969. Fine matt-finished rosewood, leather-covered cushions.
Vico Magistretti. "Caori" table. 1969. Black aluminum, base painted black. Manufactured by Knoll International.
This group, as well as the fireplace wall of

rough cement, speaks a formal language that is already post-International Style. Overemphasis of construction and material eventually led to mannerism, which soon became the fashion in architecture and furniture design.

332

333

334

333. Arne Jacobsen. Office of the City Engineer in Glostrup City Hall. 1958. Chair and sofa with bases of chrome-plated steel tubing, attached cushions. Manufactured by Fritz Hansens Eft.

Arne Jacobsen's buildings, furniture, and appliances are characterized by their finely studied detail. His furniture, usually designed for administration buildings or hotels, was often later produced for residential use.

334. Arne Jacobsen and Niels Jørgen Haugesen. "Djob" office-furniture program. 1969–70. Table bases and legs aluminum sections; table tops, drawers, and cabinets of wood coated in dark blue or ocher. Manufactured by Scandinavian Office Organisation, Ltd.

335. Poul Kjaerholm. Sofa. 1958. ▷ Chrome-plated metal base, seat, back, armrests, and feather cushions covered with leather. Manufactured by Kold Christensen.

335

336. Poul Kjaerholm. Chair. 1956. Base of
chrome-plated flat section steel with wicker
seat. Manufactured by Kold Christensen.
"Kjaerholm's chairs are characterized by a
great formal simplicity that is in complete
harmony with the materials used."[50]

336

attraction in the early fifties to a Europe that was still slowly recovering from the
devastation of the war. The tremendous influence of the United States on the entire
Western world soon brought with it a renaissance of the International Style in the
countries of its origin, where rapidly growing affluence assured a warm welcome for
cool Neo-Functionalism. In furniture showrooms all over the world homely Danish
teak began to rub elbows with polished chrome, and the imitations of Mies chairs
began to run into the hundreds. The International Style began to move out of the
office and into the home—particularly in Germany, Italy, and the Scandinavian
countries. And as affluence grew, so did the demand for quality.

This process was slower in Germany than in other countries, however. After total
defeat and the destruction of all the large cities, it took a long time until Germany
could start thinking about anything except filling its most basic needs. Contemporary
furniture began to go on sale in the fifties, under the auspices of such state-supported
programs as WK (Wohnkultur) in Germany and SW (Soziales Wohnen) in Austria,
but it was not a complete success. Inexpensive, functional furniture, based on that of
the pioneering thirties, turned out to be no match for the new Historicism that came
with the postwar economic boom and appealed to white and blue collar alike. One
reason for this new conservatism may lie in the fact that now, for the first time, cheap
travel made it possible for thousands of Europeans to see—and imitate—the art and
furniture of countries other than their own; whatever the case, the result was the

337

337. Hans Gugelot. "M 125" modular group. 1953. Manufactured by Wilhelm Bofinger.
Versatile unit furniture of metal rods; shelves and sides coated with light-gray plastic, with trim in dark afromosia wood.
The elements can be used to make any number of combinations—chests of drawers, wardrobes, bookcases, wall shelves, room dividers—for living room, bedroom, or studio. Gugelot's program is typical of the development of neo-Functionalist furniture—the attempt to utilize simple systems to articulate wall surfaces and divide rooms. The furniture industry has turned out countless variations of it.

kitsch that now began to be popularized by weekly magazines and television, in complete disregard of contemporary needs.

In the field of building, too, it was not the principles of the Bauhaus, the insights of the Weissenhof Project, or the social concern of the Frankfurt experiments that were taken up by postwar contractors, but the bungalows of the Hitler era—in the last resort little more than scaled-down versions of English country houses of the type that had dominated the suburbs of German cities since Muthesius's day. Though the great postwar demand for furniture did bring increased production, its goals were by no means primarily social, functional, or even aesthetic; the main criterion seemed to be that each year's new furniture make last year's look as outmoded as possible. Not until the acute housing shortage had finally been met did truly new ideas in home furnishings begin to appear.

Developments ran a different course in Denmark, where Arne Jacobsen's desire "to do it a little better" in design brought International Style furniture before a large public, and with it an important alternative to the dominant Teak Style (Plates 333, 334). The work of Poul Kjaerholm (born in 1929) and Jørn Utzon (born in 1918) might also be said to belong to this camp (Plates 335, 336, 338, 339). A latter-day German contribution to the theory of International Style furniture was made at the Hochschule für Gestaltung in Ulm, one of whose most distinguished members was Hans Gugelot (1920–65, Plate 337). At this design school, questions of aesthetics were given equal importance with investigations into the problems of contemporary society.

By the early sixties the International Style had begun to lose impetus. Accusations of rigidity and lifelessness were heard, particularly in connection with Mies van der Rohe's architecture. His principle of honesty of construction was taken to extremes by Brutalism, soon to be followed by mannerist and formalist variations. These trends have had an adverse effect on furniture design, with the result that no truly new formal ideas have come out of the International Style for the past ten or fifteen years. And, as so often happens at the close of a great epoch of style, people have attempted

338. Jørn Utzon. Portable furniture system. ▷ 1968. Aluminum base (triangular-section pipe in nine different sizes). Manufactured by Fritz Hansens Eft.
This series includes chairs, chaise longues, stools, and tables, as well as two- and three-seat sofas, which can also be connected to form rows. The padding is foam rubber covered with leather or fabric; the table tops are plastic-coated.

339. Jørn Utzon. Chair and footstool. ▷ 1969. Molded plywood, chrome-plated steel-tubing base, foam-rubber padding, fabric covering. Manufactured by Fritz Hansens Eft.
Utzon's chairs, which stand at the end of a stylistic development, attempt to introduce new, plastically imaginative formal elements.

338

to fill the vacuum by turning to the past. Following the successful revival of Mies, Breuer, and Le Corbusier furniture from the thirties, designs that were never conceived for mass production are being resuscitated—chairs by Mackintosh and Gaudí, pieces by Hoffmann and Strnad—in a new wave of Historicism. Basically this process represents a reaction in all fields of design to a cold and austere Functionalism. And when we remember that Functionalism had degenerated to little more than a fashion in the International Style of the postwar period, it is really no wonder that a reaction has set in.

339

New Ideas from Italy

By the onset of the sixties, European postwar reconstruction had largely run its course, and European industry had recovered lost ground to reach unprecedented levels of production The furniture business was no exception. Now the stage was set for an independent European contribution to postwar design. As their starting point, many designers naturally chose the polished forms and advanced technology of American avant-garde furniture companies; others, the solid Teak Style of Scandinavia. Within a very short time European firms had begun to make their own, highly original contributions, aided by designers who, at schools such as the Royal College of Art in London or the Hochschule für Gestaltung in Ulm, had received a thorough training not only in art but in theory, too—including other, related disciplines such as sociology.

After the demise of the International Style and the gradual ebb of the teak wave, Italy took over the lead in European furnituremaking. The style that emerged there was actually the last truly national furniture style in the narrower sense; with most barriers to world trade down and export markets expanding after the war, national currents had soon merged into one broad stream. Modern Italian furniture owed its inception to an astonishingly liberal cooperation among big business, small workshops, and progressive designers—and most particularly to the transformation that had taken place over the entire spectrum of industrial design due to the pioneering work of a number of concerned architects. The center of this dynamic development was Milan and environs, with its traditional concentration of small furniture companies.

Italy's success in this field goes back to the attempts of Italian architects to catch up with developments in central Europe during the twenties and thirties. As we know, by the late twenties the hopeful aim of Constructivism, to carry good design into all areas of life, had been smothered in the Soviet Union by an almost bourgeois conservatism, and German architecture under Hitler had turned to Classicism on a gigantic scale; yet the young architects of the modern movement in Italy, though they also were forced almost completely out of the building trade, were able to take advantage of the comparative laxness of Italian Fascism and direct their creative energies elsewhere—to home furnishings, for instance, *arredamento*. Their first designs for furniture made of steel tubing, the revival of the Chiavari chair in 1933 by Emanuele Rambaldi (Plate 59), and the many excellent prototypes for industrial

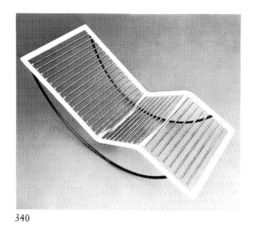

340

340. Franco Albini. Rocking chair. 1940. Iron. Collection the designer.

341. Agnoldomenico Pica. Chair. 1933. Steel tubing. Collection the designer.

342. Giuseppe Terragni. Chair. c. 1935–36. Steel and wood. Terragni collection, Como.

341

342

345. Giovanni Pintori. Poster for Olivetti ▷ typewriter. 1940. Collection the designer. Pintori, who began working as a commercial artist for Olivetti in 1936, created the company's new advertising style with his campaign for the "Studio 42." Marcello Nizzoli had been commissioned by Camillo Olivetti to find a new shape for the Summa typewriter as early as 1931. With his designs for the Lexicon 80 (1948) and Lettera 22 (1950) and their fine balance between mechanism and housing, he had a decisive influence on the later development of office typewriters.

343. Franco Albini. Radio mounted between two pieces of plate glass. 1936. Collection the designer.

"The furnishings designed by architects, generally for apartments and offices, had an important function—on the one hand in influencing public taste and on the other in changing over from hand to industrial production. These interiors were usually not conceived as single pieces, nor as combinations of one-of designs; rather, every piece of furniture that was to be manufactured—even if only one example at first—already had the character of an industrial product. Emphasis on fitness for purpose and utility, intensive study of the economy of materials and manufacturing methods, the desire to create series that were 'fun'—all of this prefigures the concepts that characterize industrial design today" (Franco Albini).[51]

344. Luigi Figini and Gino Pollini. Design for a combination radio and record player. Made in 1933 for the Società Nazionale del Grammofono.

345

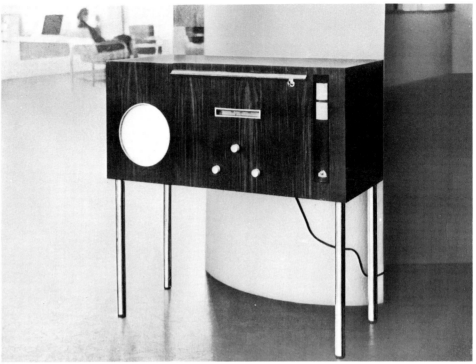

344

products of all kinds were milestones that survived the Fascist period and the war (Plates 340–344). The ongoing exchange of ideas with progressive architects and designers from all over the world who met at the Milan Triennials before and after the war gave Italian design a big impetus, as did the consistent modernity of magazines such as *Domus* and *Casabella*.

After the war, architects initially concentrated their efforts on rebuilding residential areas, and especially on raising the standards both of apartment buildings and of their furnishings. In the field of industrial design, a number of extremely fine products soon appeared which, for a country that until a short time ago had offered no advanced training in design, were truly phenomenal: the Olivetti typewriters by Marcello Nizzoli (Plate 345), and the Vespa and Lambretta motorscooters of 1948 and 1949. These models of good design were to have a wide effect, even on the shape of home furnishings.

As the Milan Triennial shows came to be dominated less and less by artists, and more and more by designers during the fifties—and when the Milan department store, La Rinascente, began awarding its *Compasso d'oro* prize for functional, modern furniture—one could say that modern design had found wide acceptance among the Italian people. Yet this acceptance was relative, as can be seen by the fact that, of the abundance of great designs produced at that time and given worldwide publicity in the specialized press, only a handful ever went into production (Plates 346–349).

Though these demanding designs were turned out in only limited numbers and reached only the happy few who could afford them, the effect they had on the rest of Europe was tremendous. Everyone began talking about the success of Italian products. What was exciting about them was their new aesthetic approach, which led to sculptural solutions that stood in direct contradiction to the rigorous functionalism of the International Style.

These new Italian products often possessed a wonderful formal logic, were sometimes spontaneous and playful, but were invariably convincing and marked by strong individualism. Yet as social considerations began to gain in importance, and designers realized that they had to take the needs of broad sections of the population

346

347

348

346. Luisa Castiglioni and Margherita Mori. Living room with bookcase, work table, and chaise longue. c. 1950. Manufactured by Ettore Canali.

347. Angelo Mangiarotti. Bookcase, fitted together of separate wooden elements. 1955. Manufactured by Fratelli Frigerio.

348. Franco Albini, Luigi Colombini, and Enzio Sgrelli. Armchair. c. 1950. Movable seat and back, foam-rubber padding. Manufactured by La Rinascente.

349. Angelo Mangiarotti. Wardrobe, built up of various-sized elements. c. 1950.
"We must begin by saying that up to 1946, the tradition of Italian design had been completely formed and developed along the lines of a culture closely linked to architecture. This, of course, was Rationalist architecture, which after 1945 became firmly associated on an ideological plane with the politically anti-Fascist movements of national liberation, and with a strong tradition, centered especially in Milan. It was still internationalist and elitist, and was at the time concerned with the problems of standard elements and prefabrication" (Vittorio Gregotti).[52]

349

350

351

350. Franco Albini and Franca Helg. Armchair. 1960. Base steel tubing, foam-rubber padding. Manufactured by Poggi.

351. Osvaldo Borsani. Armchair. 1961. Flexible metal frame, foam-rubber padding, covered with fabric, plastic, or leather. Manufactured by Tecno.

352. Marco Zanuso and Richard Sapper. Armchair. 1964. Metal frame. Manufactured by Arflex.
Seat and back of fabric or leather are connected by a hinge. The seat is adjustable to four different positions. The plastic articulation of this chair has brought about a ''play of forms'' that goes beyond the ideas of Rationalist architecture. ''While the best English products show a perfect balance between demand and solution, between result and execution, and while American products generally fill the narrow gap that the network of a perfectionist technology and a perfected production system leaves open to them, Italian design is characterized, generally speaking, by formally satisfying solutions. It is capable of suddenly producing a brilliant aesthetic solution that fills the gaps in a production in which stage of development and technique are often unmatched, which, in terms of technology and organization, is still basically coming of age, and which, as far as methods go, often resorts to improvisation'' (Vittorio Gregotti).[53]

into account in the design process, they began to leave the path of original, highly individual furniture for a limited buying public. In this period fall the first experiments with plastic as a material for furniture—by Joe Colombo and Angelo Mangiarotti in 1960 and Marco Zanuso in 1964—which it was hoped would pave the way to making good furniture at reasonable prices, and thus bring modern design to a wide audience. It was plastic furniture, technologically interesting and inexpensive to produce, that brought Italian design to international attention.

An abundance of talents, most of them architects and designers, such as Gae Aulenti, Rodolfo Bonetto, Achille and Pier Giacomo Castiglioni, Angelo Mangiarotti, Enzio Mari, Giancarlo Piretti, Alberto Rosselli, Tobia and Afra Scarpa—in addition to those named in the illustrations—helped spark a development that was diverse and multi-faceted, very much in the tradition of Mediterranean thought (Plates 350–359).

352

353. Marco Zanuso and Richard Sapper. Children's chair. 1964. Low-pressure polyethylene. Manufactured by Kartell.
This chair consists of three elements—seat, legs, and grid—which are pressure-fitted to each other. It was developed for kindergartens and first-grade classes and may also be used to build "castles" like the one illustrated.

354. Vico Magistretti. "Selene" stacking chair. 1968. Fiberglass-reinforced polyester. Manufactured by Studio Artemide.

355. Joe C. Colombo. Stacking chair. 1965. Moplen plastic. Manufactured by Kartell.

356. Carlo Viganò. Modular cabinet series. 1968. Painted wood. Manufactured by Cesare Augusto Nava.
The individual containers can be put together out of six basic elements, combined horizontally or vertically, and fitted with various dividers depending on the use to which they are to be put.

353

354

355

356

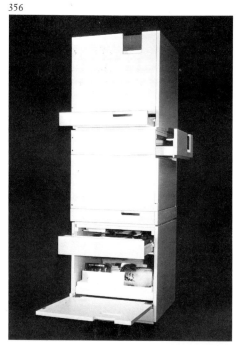

357

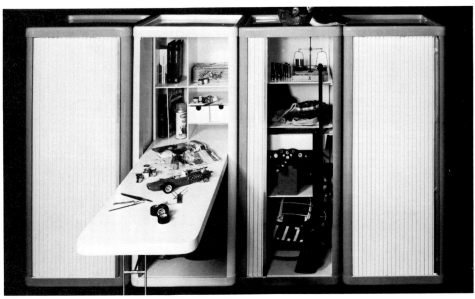

358

359

357. Anna Castelli Ferrieri. Round plastic containers. 1970. With or without sliding doors and casters, to be combined in various ways. Manufactured by Kartell.

358, 359. Pierluigi Molinari. "Box System." 1970. Manufactured by Asnaghi Rinaldo & Figli.
Low cabinets with sliding shutters. Made of plastic in two heights, they can be combined in any number of ways. Their interiors are variable—shelves, drawers, clothes rods, and also a folding desk are available. Tables can also be suspended between two cabinets on metal hangers.
"Inside these pieces of furniture, which therefore became mere equipped 'containers'—ordinary boxes—are placed all the other elements that have been invented to supply as efficiently as possible the traditional catalogue of needs our industrial-productive society has drawn up one by one" (Ettore Sottsass).[54]

At the height of this development, marked by The Museum of Modern Art exhibition, "Italy: The New Domestic Landscape," stands an attempt to bridge a gap that is wider in Italy than in many other countries—the gap between rich and poor, between production and society—by means of social-critical, and even radical and utopian projects. In the end, what many Italian designers are attempting to do now is replace design by anti-design.

Plastic Furniture

The first sketches for pressure-molded chairs in bucket form, designed to be made completely of plastic, were made in the year 1946, by Mies van der Rohe, who at that time was working and teaching in Chicago (Plate 360). Knoll and Miller went on to produce plastic furniture in the following years, but the new material was used only for the seat shells and not for the frames, which were still of metal.

The first attempts of Italian firms and designers to solve the technical and formal problems involved in plastic molding go back to the small appliances they created during the late fifties. At this early, experimental stage, designers' imagination and entrepreneurial risk were devoted to a development whose success was by no means certain. Though many of the products made at that time may appear improvised or even primitive to us today, we should not forget the basic principle that lay behind them: that of furniture as a formal unity, to be manufactured if possible by a single step of production, and of man-made material.

Both form and technique had to be evolved from the new material. Plastic, with its almost total malleability, demanded a new aesthetic; finding that aesthetic was both aided and complicated by the fact that the chemical industry was continually improving and adapting plastics to the needs of furnituremaking. Designers now had a material at hand with which chairs could be form-fitted to the human body with comparative simplicity. Their models were like sculptures, and their imaginations were limited only by the requirements of machine production and the characteristics of the material. Plastic chairs and small tables, often stackable (Plates 353–355, 361, 363), were particularly attractive to consumers because of their low weight and generally low price—and technical improvements and larger production runs would lower the price even more. Other advantages of plastic for furniture—shock and scratch resistance and brilliant color—are in continual process of improvement.

The designers of northern Europe, like many of their colleagues in other countries, began to tire of the Teak Style around the mid-sixties and turned to experiments in plastic. Soon it was an international trend. Nevertheless, thanks to the variety of models on sale, their precise execution, and their convincing formal quality, Italy still remained the unique and often-copied ideal.

When it came to shelves and cabinets of plastic, manufacturers soon ran into technical difficulties that put strict limits on size (Plate 357). Though its excellent sculptural qualities made it ideal for seating, plastic proved to be inferior to wood or metal when it came to constructing the rectilinear forms of this type of furniture. As in so many areas of design, here again function proved to be the limiting factor. Successful solutions were found in some cases, for instance where small, single elements can be put together to make larger units, as in the shelves illustrated (Plates 361, 362).

Plastic furniture, if it is to be produced in large quantities as a popularly priced article, has to be manufactured industrially from start to finish. Thus its technical and formal development will have to be accompanied by detailed marketing research.

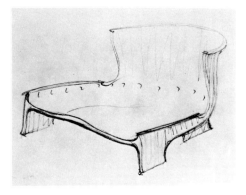

360. Mies van der Rohe. Design of a seat shell to be made of plastic. 1946.
This visionary sketch by Mies van der Rohe reveals the malleability and technical possibilities of plastic—particularly when reinforced at critical points—but it also shows up its limitations.

361

361. Vico Magistretti. Table, with detachable legs; chairs. 1969 and 1971. Reinforced fiberglass. Manufactured by Artemide.
Ernesto Gismondi. "Dodona 300" shelf system. 1971. ABS resin; sides and shelves are connected by hidden metal angles. Manufactured by Studio Artemide.

362. Corrado Cocconi and Fabio Lenci. Shelf system with Plexiglas cubes. 1970. Fittings and connecting pieces chrome-plated metal, base polished aluminum and black Plexiglas. Manufactured by Ilform.

362

363. Jürgen Lange. "behr 1600" wall unit. Built up of separate components on a module system that is variable in height, width, and depth. The sides are drilled to take shelves and drawer elements. Folding beds and tables are available, as are doors and back walls when the unit is to be used as a room divider. Manufactured by Behr Produktion KG.

In the foreground:

Mario Bellini. "Amanta" stacking table. 1967. Plastic. Manufactured by C & B Italia. Verner Panton. Stacking chair. 1960–68. Fiberglass and polyester, breakproof and weather-resistant. Manufactured by Herman Miller, Inc.

"When production facilities start turning out mass products with the goal of increasing profits, mass consumption must be assured. That is why corporations today are forced to create markets."[55]

Design, manufacture, and sales of plastic furniture obey the laws of industrial society, perhaps more than any other type of furniture to date. If it is conceived to serve its function, designed to please the eye, and offered at prices that all can afford, plastic furniture may provide us with a way to bring modern design to a wider audience than ever before.

364

From Chairs and Tables to Domestic Landscape

Since the Baroque period it had been common practice for the upper class to commission architects to design not only houses but the furniture to go with them, or at the very least to entrust the job to skilled craftsmen. From the mid-nineteenth century on, when European cities started to grow and apartment buildings began to go up, the middle class has generally tried to emulate this aristocratic ideal. Furniture manufacturers of the day, not yet working on a full division-of-labor basis and not yet completely industrialized, offered a large choice of furniture in various historical styles proportioned to fit the rooms of the new apartments. As industrialization progressed, copies of antique furniture and, later, Art Nouveau designs that had been adapted for limited production began to take up more and more space in furniture-manufacturers' catalogues. This type of furniture is still common today; sets or ensembles—usually consisting of a couch, two armchairs, and a coffee table—are a standard item in the industry, as a glance into almost any retailer's display window will show. Meant to reflect a high social status, these sets are generally much too large and bulky for today's apartments and take up valuable space. Nonetheless, they dominate a large sector of the furniture market.

Our own century has seen increasing specialization in the furniture industry, with some companies making only certain product lines, such as combination wall

364. A living room.
The furniture here, from very different historical periods with very different ideas of style, is a good example of the unorthodox interiors of the seventies. Not stylistic dogmatism but free choice (and good taste) are the best assurance of a pleasant and livable home environment.

365. Jürgen Lange. "behr 1600 paneel" program. 1970–71. Manufactured by Behr Produktion KG.
Shelves, box elements, mirrors, and tables may be suspended from the uprights of this wall unit wherever they are needed. The "fauteuil grand confort" by Le Corbusier (see Plate 252), designed fifty years earlier, fits perfectly into these surroundings.

cabinets, seating, or kitchen furnishings. During the past few decades, under the pressure of automation and large production runs, there has been a counter-tendency, which has led to dividing up interiors into their component parts once again. An example may make this clear; cabinets, chests of drawers, and bookcases, in the course of their integration into wall-filling combinations that reach from floor to ceiling, have become more and more autonomous, to the point of being almost architectonic elements in space. In front of them the other furniture, especially chairs, looks almost like carefully positioned props on a stage (Plate 365).

This tendency toward fixed placement and diversity of style has been subjected to a great deal of criticism lately. Rather than interiors that reflect the owner's status, many designers today are out to create "total environments." The key word here is variability, and the idea is to do away with one-purpose rooms with one-purpose furniture and to create surroundings amenable to new life styles and informal behavior. You do not sit on chairs in these environments; you lie down, make yourself comfortable, and enjoy your freedom from convention—generally on cushions spread around the room, sculpted foam-rubber seats, and wall-to-wall carpets (Plates 366–370). This trend to free and versatile utilization of the entire available floor space certainly contains a large dose of criticism of those perfectly planned interiors which, once they have been installed, are fixed for evermore.

Suggestions of the type made at the Cologne Furniture Fairs by designers such as

366

Verner Panton (born in 1926), Joe C. Colombo (1930–71), and Olivier Mourgue (born in 1939), for the Bayer Corporation's *Visiona* stands, actually were meant as eye-catchers, to show people what could be done with modern plastics (Plates 371–373). It was not long, however, until these "domestic landscapes" were picked up by designers, usually in miniature, easy-to-make versions, and the interest of the furniture companies was aroused. The foam-filled cushions, which go well with simple shelves and tables in wood or plastic, have proved particularly popular with the younger generation. Domestic landscapes of this kind work best in apartments with open floor plans.

368–370. Joe C. Colombo. "Additional ▷ System" seating program. 1969. Manufactured by Sormani.
Slices of foam rubber in six different sizes, covered with elastic material and attached to a metal bar to give chairs or couches of any shape and length desired. A small multi-purpose plastic table completes the ensemble.
"The problem today is to offer furnishings that are basically autonomous, that is, independent of their architectonic housing and so coordinatable and programmable that they can be adapted to every present and future space situation" (Joe Colombo).[56]

◁ 366. A spacious living room in a private American home .
The U-shaped sunken couch replaces almost all portable furniture.

367

367. Living room with freely grouped seating elements .
Different versions of a domestic landscape. In the first, with its sunken couch before the fireplace, the room dominates; yet the furniture is so fixed that no flexibility in the use of space—as in Japanese houses—can occur. The second solution, by Joe Colombo, starts from the idea of flexibility and variability within a completely open plan. Not only the grouping of the elements but their use, whether for sitting or reclining, is left up to the user's imagination.

368

369

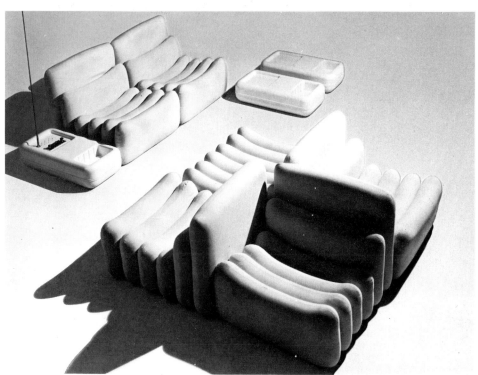

370

371

371. Joe C. Colombo. Kitchen box block. A fully furnished, air-conditioned kitchen for "Wohnmodell 1969" at "Visiona 69," an exhibition by Bayer AG of Leverkusen at the International Furniture Fair, Cologne, 1969.

372

372. Joe C. Colombo. Central living block for "Wohnmodell 1969."

The raised, square center has cushions for sitting and reclining and a bar in the middle; above it, suspended from the ceiling, is a round, revolving bookcase with a television set, which can also be turned 360 degrees. In the background, the sleeping cell ("night cell block") with bathroom and shelf space. The entire block is hermetically sealed and air-conditioned.

"It is a semi-functioning prototype meant to demonstrate a suggested new way of living; it is a structure made of three machines that are coordinated with one another and serve to create a new world to live in" (Joe Colombo).[57]

373. Olivier Mourgue. "Wohnmodell 1972." At "Visiona 72," an exhibition of Bayer AG of Leverkusen at the International Furniture Fair, Cologne, 1972.
"An open, undivided living space in which the entire life of the family takes place, a common living area that adapts to every change (birth of children, older children moving out, etc.).... Variability of space, natural freedom of movement, bringing nature into the interior, for instance with a soft floor covering that resembles moss and earth...."[58]

Education As a Chance for the Future

Against the compulsion of consumer society to subject every product to rapid changes in fashion stands the desire of a small but continually growing number of people to escape from this pressure and to become actively involved in creating their own, personal home environments. Yet a walk through any furniture fair, be it in Paris, Cologne, or Milan, should be enough to rob anyone of his illusions with respect to the true situation in the furniture market. It is safe to say that most furniture companies and retailers (not to mention most buyers) still prefer styles inspired by the past—prettily painted "peasant" furniture, for instance—perhaps as a way of compensating for the missing warmth in their daily lives. Rather than good contemporary designs, the stores offer fake Baroque, Spanish rustic, and the glib forms of a noncommittal modern. Good modern furniture has been granted only a very modest corner in our civilization.

The interiors of tomorrow will not come without some serious rethinking in the field of city planning. What is needed in the face of our rapidly disappearing countryside is an industrialized program of housing, based on higher population density and offering apartments with open floor plans. The greatest possible variability and mobility for every individual are just as important as the chance to design and plan one's own surroundings—in a word, participation in the design of housing, under the guidance of trained architects and planners.

An urban environment conceived in this way, modest but well designed, will require furniture that is not sensational but useful, and above all flexible. It should be simple and human in form and designed for manufacture in large numbers at a low price. Furniture is basically always a child of its time, if only because the demands

374

375

376

374, 375. Alberto Rosselli with Abe Kozo. "Pack 1" portable folding chair. 1975. Shell canvas, cushions foam plastic with dacron covering. Manufactured by Bonacina.

377

376, 377. Günter Sulz. "Canvas" seating combination. 1973. Inflated plastic cushions with canvas covering in various colors. Seat, back, and sides are held together with rope. Manufactured by Behr + Sulz.

378, 379. Maurizio Dallasta and Davide Mercatali. "Nomade" chair. 1975. Five cushions are buckled together to form a chair; other combinations are also possible. The cushions are covered with cotton fabric or canvas. Manufactured by Donchi Formart.

378

380. Piero Gatti, Cesare Paolini, Franco Teodoro. Seat bag. 1969. Leather. The bag is filled with plastic pearls that adapt to every body position, and is light and easy to carry. Manufactured by Zanotta.

Our age requires seating that is versatile and light, to complement the relaxed clothing and life styles of the seventies. Light chairs and portable cushions make for comfort—whether you sit, recline, or lie down on them.

379

380

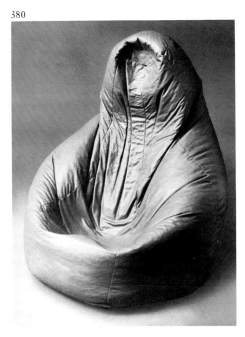

that people make on it change—and they often change several times even in the course of our own lifetime. Nonetheless, this process should not be subject to the dictates of fashion alone.

Then, too, many young people today establish their households with very modest means. Having grown up in a rapidly shrinking world, they are accustomed to living in one apartment or city today and in another tomorrow. Rigid tradition has given way to a new, flexible life style that, though it may express a greater social equality than ever before, is also characterized by an extremely individual view of interiors as personal environments. Light, versatile furniture makes it possible to furnish even today's tiny apartments in a pleasing way, even on a limited budget.

The variable furniture systems that have recently come on the market, often sold cash-and-carry to be assembled at home, are a good example of the kind of policy that is needed for the future. They provide an excellent means of supplementing, at a reasonable price, those single pieces, which by reason of their aesthetic quality and their craftsmanship may still form the center of gravity in any good contemporary interior.

Home furnishings of this type, if they are to be successful in the long run, will

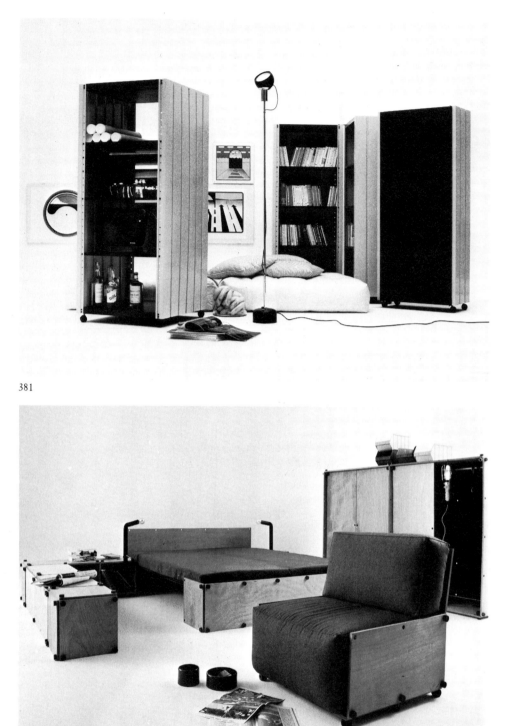

381

382

Examples of furniture to be assembled by the buyer himself from a wide range of available elements, and changed or added to at will. The material—whether wood, metal, or plastic—is no longer as important as low price and high variability. Individualistic furnishings not only typify our highly mobile society; they show that a need exists to create one's own personal environment in a world dominated by technology and conformity.

probably have to be accompanied by a program of consumer education. As long as most people's idea of formal quality swings back and forth between the poles of Historicism and *kitsch,* a truly human and generally valid formal quality in home furnishings, as in architecture itself, will remain the dream of a few. There is reason to hope that a program of education in home furnishing, starting in the schools, might help people get over their status-consciousness and need for representation in choosing the objects they live with. If the mass media were to do their part, and if good, simple modern furniture is made available at reasonable prices, then a change may truly come about.

An architecture of quiet is going to have to follow the chaos of form and material of

383

our consumer age, if we wish to continue existing reasonably with technology. Simple spaces for living, with clean, well-designed furniture, will go far toward placing man in the center of his world again.

383. Günter Renkel. "Robinson" program. 1976. Solid pine. The basic element here is the wide ladders, on the rungs of which beds, bookshelves, desks, and drawers are suspended. Manufactured by ZE Möbel, Einrichtungsbedarf GmbH & Co. KG.

Notes

1. In Franz Glück, ed., *Adolf Loos—Sämtliche Schriften in zwei Bänden,* vol. 1, p. 440 f. (Vienna and Munich: Verlag Herold, 1962).

2. Otto Johannsen, *Geschichte des Eisens* (Düsseldorf: Verlag Stahleisen GmbH, 1953).

3. New York: Oxford University Press, 1948.

4. London: Faber and Faber, 1952.

5. Quoted from a sales catalogue of the Thonet Company, 1911.

6. In Wilhelm Franz Exner, *Das Biegen des Holzes* (Leipzig: Verlag B.F. Voigt, 1922).

7. Wend Fischer, "Gestaltungsweise und Lebensform—zum Funktionalismus der Shaker," from the exhibition catalogue *Die Shaker,* Die Neue Sammlung, Munich, 1974.

8. *Ibid.*

9. In Leonardo Benevolo, *Geschichte der Architektur des 19. und 20. Jahrhunderts,* vol. 1 (Munich: Verlag Georg D. Callwey, 1964).

10. Nikolaus Pevsner, "Hochviktorianisches Kunstgewerbe," in *Architektur und Design* (Munich: Prestel Verlag, 1971).

11. Barbara Morris, "Morris und Company," in *Du* (Zurich), vol. 25 (September 1965).

12. In Nikolaus Pevsner, *Wegbereiter der modernen Formgebung* (Reinbeck: Rowohlt Verlag, 1957). (Nikolaus Pevsner, *Pioneers of Modern Design.* The Museum of Modern Art, New York, 1949.)

13. In Leonardo Benevolo, *op. cit.*

14. Nikolaus Pevsner. *Architektur und Design, op. cit.*

15. In Julius Posener, *Anfänge des Funktionalismus, von Arts and Crafts zum Deutschen Werkbund* (Berlin: Ullstein Verlag [Bauwelt Fundamente 11], 1964).

16. In Nikolaus Pevsner. *Architektur und Design, op. cit.*

17. *Ibid.*

18. Arthur Heygate Mackmurdo, *Wren's City Churches* (Orpington, Kent, 1883).

19. In *The Studio* (London), vol. XVI, 1899.

20. Henri van de Velde. *Geschichte meines Lebens* (Munich: R. Piper & Co., 1962).

21. In Klaus Jürgen Sembach, "Möbel," *Jugendstil—Der Weg ins 20. Jahrhunderts* (Munich: Keyser'sche Verlagsbuchhandlung, 1959).

22. "Prairie Architecture," in *Modern Architecture* (The Kahn Lectures). (Princeton: Princeton University Press, 1931).

23. Quoted in *Frank Lloyd Wright—Schriften und Bauten* (Munich and Vienna: Langen-Müller Verlag, 1963).

24. In "Prairie Architecture," *op. cit.*

25. In *Adolf Loos—Sämtliche Schriften, op. cit.*

26. "Josef Veillich" (1929), in *Adolf Loos—Sämtliche Schriften, op. cit.*

27. In Julius Posener, *Anfänge des Funktionalismus, op. cit.*

28. Hermann Muthesius. *Wie baue ich mein Haus* (Munich: F. Bruckmann, 1917).

29. Erich Boltenstern. *Wiener Möbel.* (Stuttgart: Julius Hoffmann Verlag, 1934).

30. H.L.C. Jaffé, *De Stijl, 1971–1931. Der niederländische Beitrag zur modernen Kunst* (Berlin: Ullstein, 1965).

31. *Ibid.*

32. Paul Overy. *De Stijl* (New York: Studio Vista/Dutton Pictureback, 1969).

33. *Marcel Breuer, 1921–1962* (Stuttgart: Verlag Gerd Hatje, 1962).

34. Walter Gropius, *Bauhausbauten Dessau* (vol. 12 of the Bauhausbücher) (Munich: Albert Langen Verlag, 1930).

35. First published by W.W. Norton, New York, 1932.

36. In Le Corbusier and Pierre Jeanneret, *Oeuvre complète, 1910–1929.* W. Boesiger and O. Stonorov, eds. (Zurich: Verlag Girsberger, 1960), p. 105.

37. From an article in *Rote Fahne* (Berlin), May 1, 1927.

38. Walter Müller-Wulckow. "Die deutsche Wohnung der Gegenwart," *Die Architektur der Zwanziger Jahre in Deutschland* (Königstein: Langewiesche, 1975).

39. Elias Cornell. "Bruno Mathsson och tiden," *Arkitektur* (Stockholm), no. 3, 1967.

40. Aino and Alvar Aalto, in *Alvar Aalto* (Zurich: Verlag für Architektur, 1963).

41. *Ibid.*

42. Sigfried Giedion, "Alvar Aalto," *Architectural Review,* February 1950, pp. 77–84.

43. In *Furniture from the Design Collection,* exhibition catalogue of The Museum of Modern Art, New York, 1973.

44. From a catalogue of the Herman Miller International Collection.

45. From the introduction to the catalogue of the exhibition "Charles Eames, Furniture from the Design Collection," The Museum of Modern Art, New York, 1973.

46. From a catalogue of the Herman Miller International Collection.

47. From the catalogue of the exhibition "Charles Eames," *op. cit.*

48. From the book on the exhibition "Knoll International," Museum des 20. Jahrhunderts, Vienna, 1973.

49. *Ibid.*

50. In Jocelyn de Noblet, "Design—Introduction à l'histoire et l'évolution des formes industrielles de 1820 à aujourd'hui" (Paris: Éditions Stock, 1974).

51. In a letter to the author on Italian furniture design in the interwar period, 1972.

52. Vittorio Gregotti, "Italian Design, 1945–1971," *Italy: The New Domestic Landscape,* catalogue of The Museum of Modern Art, New York, 1972.

53. Vittorio Gregotti. "Design in Italien," *Design als Postulat am Beispiel Italien,* exhibition catalogue of Internationales Design Zentrum (IDZ), Berlin, 1973.

54. In *Italy: The New Domestic Landscape, op. cit.*

55. Caption to a figure illustrating the production of the "Panton"chair, in Bernd Löbach, *Industrial Design, Grundlagen der Produktionsgestaltung* (Munich: Verlag Karl Thiemig, 1976).

56. In *Design als Postulat am Beispiel Italien, op. cit.*

57. In *Farbe und Design,* no. 3 (Gaildorf, Württemberg: Farbe und Design Verlags GmbH).

58. In *Farbe und Design,* no. 3, *op. cit.*

Bibliography

Alison, Filippo. *Charles Rennie Mackintosh As a Designer of Chairs*. Translated by Bruno and Cristina Del Priore. London: Warehouse Publications, 1974.

Andresen, Th., and Jordan, Bitten. *Wohnen in Skandinavien*. Title and text in German, French, and English. Stuttgart: Julius Hoffman Verlag, 1958.

Andrews, Edward Deming. *Religion in Wood: A Book of Shaker Furniture*. Bloomington, Indiana, and London: Indiana University Press, 1966.

Andrews, Edward Deming, and Andrews, Faith. *Shaker Furniture: The Craftsmanship of an American Communal Sect,* 2d ed. New Haven, Conn.: Yale University Press, 1939.

Aslin, Elizabeth. *Nineteenth-Century English Furniture*. New York: Thomas Yoseloff, 1962.

Beer, Eileene Harrison. *Scandinavian Design: Objects of a Life Style*. New York: Farrar, Straus and Giroux and The American-Scandinavian Society, 1975.

Bermpohl, R., and Winkelmann, H. *Das Möbelbuch*. Gütersloh, West Germany: C. Bertelsmann Verlag, 1958.

Bishop, Robert. *Centuries and Styles of the American Chair, 1640–1970*. New York: E. P. Dutton & Co., 1972.

Boger, Louise Ade. *Furniture Past & Present: A Complete Illustrated Guide to Furniture Styles from Ancient to Modern*. Garden City, N.Y.: Doubleday & Co., 1966.

Bossaglia, Rossana. *Art Nouveau: Revolution in Interior Design*. New York: Crown Publishers, Crescent Books, 1973.

Ditzel, Nanna, and Ditzel, Jørgen, eds. *Danish Chairs*. Title and text in Danish and English. N.p.: Høst & Søns Forlag, 1954; distributed in the United States by Wittenborn and Company, New York.

Drexler, Arthur, and Daniel, Greta. *Introduction to Twentieth-Century Design from the Collection of the Museum of Modern Art*. N.p., n.d.; distributed by Doubleday & Co., Garden City, N.Y., 1959.

Frey, Gilbert. *The Modern Chair: 1850 to Today*. Title and text in English, French, and German. New York: Architectural Book Publishing Co., 1970.

Fry, Charles Rahn, ed. *Art Deco Interiors in Color*. New York: Dover Publications, 1977.

Fusco, Renato de. *Le Corbusier designer: i moboli del 1929*. Milan: Casabella, 1976; distributed in the United States by Rizzoli International Publications, New York.

Glaeser, Ludwig. *Ludwig Mies van der Rohe: Furniture and Furniture Drawings from the Design Collection and Mies van der Rohe Archive, the Museum of Modern Art, New York*. New York: The Museum of Modern Art, 1977.

Hald, Arthur, and Skawonius, Sven Erik. *Contemporary Swedish Design*. New York: Pellegrini & Cudahy; Stockholm: Nordisk Rotogravyr, 1951.

Hård af Segerstad, Ulf. *Modern Scandinavian Furniture*. Translated by Nancy and Edward Maze. Totowa, N.J.: Bedminster Press, 1963.

Haweis, E[liza]. *The Art of Decoration*. London: Chatto and Windus, 1889. Reprint. New York: Garland Publishing, 1977.

Hiort, Esbjørn. *Modern Danish Furniture*. Title and text in English, French, German, and Danish. Translated into English by Eve M. Wendt. New York: Architectural Book Publishing Co., n.d.

Howarth, Thomas. *Charles Rennie Mackintosh and the Modern Movement*. 2d ed. London: Routledge & Kegan Paul, 1977. Reprint. New York: Garland Publishing, 1977.

Joel, David. *Furniture Design Set Free: The British Furniture Revolution from 1851 to the Present Day.* New rev. ed. London: J. M. Dent and Sons, 1969.

Kane, Patricia E. *300 Years of American Seating Furniture: Chairs and Beds from the Mabel Brady Garvan and Other Collections at Yale University.* Boston: New York Graphic Society, 1976.

Kron, Joan, and Slesin, Suzanne. *High-Tech: The Industrial Style and Source Book for the Home.* New York: Clarkson N. Potter, 1978.

Lenning, Henry F. *The Art Nouveau.* The Hague: Martinus Nijhoff, 1951.

Logie, Gordon. *Furniture from Machines.* London: George Allen and Unwin, 1947.

Madsen, S[tephan] Tschudi. *Art Nouveau.* Translated by R. I. Christopherson. New York and Toronto: McGraw-Hill Book Company, 1967.

Meader, Robert F. W. *Illustrated Guide to Shaker Furniture.* New York: Dover Publications, 1972.

Meadmore, Clement. *The Modern Chair: Classics in Production.* New York and Melbourne: Van Nostrand Reinhold Company, 1975.

Molesworth, H. D., and Kenworthy-Browne, John. *Three Centuries of Furniture in Color.* New York: Viking Press, A Studio Book, 1972.

National Collection of Fine Arts, Renwick Gallery. *Shakers: Furniture and Objects from the Faith and Edward Deming Andrews Collections Commemorating the Bicentenary of the American Shakers.* Washington, D.C.: Smithsonian Institution Press, 1973.

New York, The Museum of Modern Art. *Aalto: Architecture and Furniture.* 1938.

Noyes, Eliot F. *Organic Design in Home Furnishings.* New York: The Museum of Modern Art, 1941.

Pevsner, Nikolaus. *Pioneers of Modern Design: From William Morris to Walter Gropius.* Rev. and partly rewritten ed. New York and Harmondsworth, England: Penguin Books, 1975.

Raynsford, Julia. *The Story of Furniture.* London and New York: Hamlyn, 1975.

Rhode Island School of Design, Museum of Art. *Furniture of Today: An Exhibition Presenting a Cross-Section of Modern Furniture Now Being Manufactured.* Providence, 1948.

Ritter, Enrichetta, ed. *Italian Design: Furniture.* Title and text in Italian, English, French, and German. Translated into English by Robert Kettleson. Milan and Rome: Carlo Bestetti edizioni arte, 1968.

Saint Louis, City Art Museum of. *Product Environment: Exhibition of New Furniture.* 1970.

Selz, Peter, and Constantine, Mildred, eds. *Art Nouveau: Art and Design at the Turn of the Century.* New York: The Museum of Modern Art, 1959. Reprint. N.p.: Arno Press, 1972.

Shea, John G. *The American Shakers and Their Furniture: With Measured Drawings of Museum Classics.* New York and Melbourne: Van Nostrand Reinhold Company, 1971.

Watson, Francis, introduction by. *The History of Furniture.* New York: William Morrow & Co., 1976.

Wettergren, Erik. *The Modern Decorative Arts of Sweden.* Revised by Edward Russel. Translated by Tage Palm. Malmö, Sweden: Malmö Museum, 1926; distributed in the United States by The American-Scandinavian Foundation, New York.

Young, Dennis, and Young, Barbara. *Furniture in Britain Today.* Title and text in English, French, and German. New York: Wittenborn and Company, 1964.

Index

Page numbers are set in roman; plate numbers, in *italic*.

Photograph Credits

Photographs not credited are in the collection of the author or the publisher Gerd Hatje, Stuttgart. The numbers refer to plates.

Hélène Adant, Paris 45,47
André Adegg, Paris 362
AEG-Telefunken Firmenarchiv, Braunschweig 20
Archivo ''Amigos de Gaudí'' (Foto Aleu), Barcelona 171
Ancillotti Fotografie s.r.l., Milan 352
The Architects Collaborative, Inc., Cambridge, Mass. 197
The Architectural Press Ltd., London 9
Art et Décoration, Paris 244
Artek Oy AB., Helsinki 301–305, 307, 308, 310

James L. Ballard, Collection Susan Jackson Keig, Chicago 103
Aldo Ballo, Milan 250, 251, 353, 354, 361
Bauhaus-Archiv, Berlin 25, 216, 217, 221–223, 226–228, 230–232
Behr International, Wendlingen 330, 363, 365, 367, 376, 377
Behr + Sulz, Bietigheim 376, 377
Arturo Belloni 372
Bibliothèque Royal Albert I, Brussels 64, 142
Van den Bichelaer, Geldrop 208
Bildarchiv Foto Marburg 10, 18, 19, 143, 147, 148, 161, 165, 187, 188, 192
Walter Binder, Zurich 144
Werner Blaser, Basel 134
Wilhelm Bofinger, Ilsfeld 337
Bonacina s.r.l., Meda 374, 375, 381, 382
Marcel Breuer, New York 218, 229, 233, 237

Carlotto 249
Valerio Castelli & Carlo Chambry 357
Centrokappa, Noviglio (Milan) 355
Chicago Architectural Photographing Company 177
Lucca Chmel, Vienna 50, 72, 96, 98, 164, 179, 180, 309
Clari, Milan 368–370
Attilio del Commune, Milan 374, 375
Country Life, London 117
The Crystal Palace Exhibition, Illustrated Catalogue (1851) 46

Domus, Milan 59, 62
Donchi Formart s.r.l., Briosco (Milan) 378, 379
Dotreville, Brussels 17, 140

Fratelli Fabbri Editori, Milan 4
Finlands Nationalmuseum, Helsinki 300
Hans Finsler, Zurich 236
Wend Fischer, Munich 111
Fotorama, Milan 358, 359
France & Søn, Hillerød 290
Frank Leslie's Popular Monthly (Dec. 1885) 99, 101
Jørn Freddie, Copenhagen 295

Gemeentemuseum, Amsterdam 214
Alexandre Georges, Pomona, N.Y. 68
Photo-Atelier Gerlach, Vienna 184
Giraudon, Paris 149, 154, 155
Glöck, Karlsruhe 190
S. R. Gnamm, Munich 11, 39, 43, 49, 60, 105, 107–109, 145, 176, 191, 215, 241, 291, 292, 306
Görlich Editore, Paderno Dugnano (Milan) 61, 252
Gruppoquatro Studio, Milan 252

Sören Hallgren, Stockholm 113
Erik Hansen, Copenhagen 286
Fritz Hansens Eft., Allerød 275–279, 281, 282, 284, 285, 338, 339
Robert Haussmann, Zurich 331
Hedrich-Blessing, Chicago 238
Keld Helmer-Petersen, Copenhagen 66, 294, 336
Lucien Hervé, Paris 245, 246

Jonals Co., Copenhagen 33

Fas Keuzenkamp, Pijnacker 210
Knoll International, Murr/Murr 235, 243, 323–328, 332, 364
Mogens S. Koch, Hørsholm 288, 289
Konstflitföreningen i Finland, Helsinki 298
Kunstgewerbemuseum, Zurich 121, 139, 141, 144, 146, 153, 159, 162, 169, 182

Bella C. Landauer Collection, New-York Historical Society 13
Landesmuseum, Trier 63
Adolf Lazi, Stuttgart 254

A. Lengauer, Munich 26
Lichtbildwerkstätte Alpenland, Vienna 95, 42, 181, 183
L'Illustration, Paris 24
Dr. Lossen & Co., Stuttgart 258

A. Mangiarotti, Milan 347, 349
Gilbert Mangin, Nancy 152
MAS, Barcelona 173, 175
Karl Mathsson, Värnamo 267
Norman McGrath, New York 366
Herman Miller AG, Basel 314–322
William Morris, Bath 106
Musée des Arts Décoratifs, Paris 151
Museen der Stadt Wien 5
Museo Poldi-Pezzoli, Milan 44, 340, 342–345
Museum für Kunst und Gewerbe, Hamburg 296
Museum of Finnish Architecture (Loja Saarinen), Helsinki 299
Museum of Modern Art, The, New York 31, 53, 150, 312, 313

National Buildings Record, London 114, 116, 132
National Gallery, London 4, 41
National Monuments Record, London 124
Die Neue Sammlung, Munich 103, 111, 168, 209, 261
Horstheinz Neuendorff, Baden-Baden 67
Toni Nicolini 341

Österreichische Nationalbibliothek, Bildarchiv, Vienna 42, 95
Österreichisches Museum für angewandte Kunst, Vienna 185, 186, 203, 264

Ray Pearson, Chicago 112
Thomas Pedersen og Poul Pedersen, Århus 273
Pietinen, Helsinki 297
Roland Pletersky 69, 71, 73, 79

Robert, Barcelona 172

Oscar Savio, Rome 58
Richard Schenkirz, Leonberg 330
J. Scherb, Vienna 204
Ingrid Schindler, Vienna 203, 264
H. Schmölz, D.W.B., Cologne 353
R. Schmutz 381
Louis Schnakenburg, Copenhagen 335, 338